VOCABULARY WORDSEARCHES for Clever Kids

Buster Books

Puzzles and solutions
by Dr Gareth Moore
B.Sc (Hons) M.Phil Ph.D

Illustrations and cover
artwork by Chris Dickason

Cover Design by Angie Allison
Designed by Zoe Bradley and Jade Moore
Edited by Josephine Southon
Educational Consultancy by Kirstin Swanson

First published in Great Britain in 2022 by Buster Books,
an imprint of Michael O'Mara Books Limited,
9 Lion Yard, Tremadoc Road, London SW4 7NQ

W www.mombooks.com/buster

f Buster Books

🐦 @BusterBooks

📷 @buster_books

Clever Kids is a trade mark of Michael O'Mara Books Limited.

A CIP catalogue record for this book is available from the British Library.

ISBN: 978-1-78055-826-4

1 3 5 7 9 10 8 6 4 2

Papers used by Buster Books are natural, recyclable products made of wood from
well-managed, FSC®-certified forests and other controlled sources. The manufacturing
processes conform to the environmental regulations of the country of origin.

Printed and bound in July 2022 by CPI Group (UK) Ltd,
108 Beddington Lane, Croydon, CR0 4YY, United Kingdom.

MIX
Paper from
responsible sources
FSC
www.fsc.org FSC® C171272

INTRODUCTION

This book is full of special wordsearches that help test and build your vocabulary.

Synonym Puzzles

The first 100 puzzles are 'synonym' wordsearches. Synonyms are words or phrases that have exactly the same (or nearly the same) meaning as other words.

Each puzzle in this section starts with an example sentence, with one word written in CAPITALS. At the bottom of the page you'll see a list of synonyms of this word, which you must find in the wordsearch grid. These synonyms may be hidden in the grid in any direction, including diagonally, and may read either forwards or backwards. Some of the words might even overlap and use the same letters.

Some of the synonyms contain spaces or punctuation. Ignore the spaces or punctuation when looking in the grid, and only search for the letters.

When you find a word, mark it in the grid and cross it off the list. If you get stuck, the answers are at the back of the book.

There is space at the top of every page for you to write how long it took you to do each puzzle. There are three levels of difficulty – beginner, intermediate and advanced – but you can start on any puzzle you like!

Bonus Puzzles

Puzzles 101 to 144 are bonus puzzles, which include wordsearches. They test your knowledge of opposites, anagrams and more.

Good luck and happy searching!

BEGINNER

PUZZLE 1: SMILE

The funny joke made the girl **SMILE**.

U	B	E	A	M	A	L	G
I	S	U	L	K	K	L	U
B	M	B	L	G	N	H	L
G	I	A	N	M	G	G	U
R	R	H	L	U	R	I	R
M	K	A	A	I	H	I	G
R	H	L	N	A	B	E	U
K	E	L	K	C	U	H	C

BEAM
CHUCKLE
GIGGLE
GRIN
LAUGH
SMIRK

PUZZLE 2: JUMP

A kangaroo uses its long legs to **JUMP**.

L	O	E	K	P	H	D	U
I	L	C	E	I	N	P	B
V	E	N	E	K	P	G	D
V	A	U	N	S	N	N	A
A	P	O	B	I	U	V	O
U	R	B	R	O	H	U	L
L	P	P	B	L	N	O	O
T	S	U	S	I	R	P	P

BOUNCE   SKIP
BOUND   SPRING
HOP   VAULT
LEAP

PUZZLE 3: FLY

The butterfly opened its wings and tried to **FLY**.

D	U	T	S	K	I	F	Y
O	R	O	F	H	L	A	G
F	A	T	O	U	W	R	L
R	A	V	T	A	V	I	I
O	E	T	T	F	I	S	D
R	E	I	F	O	E	E	E
R	L	I	F	T	O	F	F
F	T	A	K	E	O	F	F

FLIT AWAY
FLUTTER
GLIDE
HOVER
LIFT OFF
RISE
SOAR
TAKE OFF

PUZZLE 4: PUT

He needed a safe place to PUT the valuable painting.

```
E   E   L   T   T   E   S   P
T   T   T   T   S   K   O   L
A   T   I   R   E   S   T   P
U   U   E   S   I   I   E   L
T   T   L   T   O   E   I   A
I   D   I   A   K   P   T   C
S   O   T   O   Y   E   E   E
N   O   T   K   I   P   I   D
```

DEPOSIT   POSITION
KEEP   REST
LAY   SETTLE
PLACE   SITUATE

PUZZLE 5: FALL

The paper plane began to **FALL**.

G	D	K	D	U	L	P	T
P	O	E	N	I	B	T	U
P	O	D	S	I	V	P	M
U	M	R	O	C	S	E	B
O	C	T	D	W	E	S	L
D	U	E	C	S	N	N	E
I	P	L	U	N	G	E	D
P	P	L	U	M	M	E	T

DESCEND
DIP
DIVE
DROP
GO DOWN
PLUMMET
PLUNGE

SINK
TUMBLE

PUZZLE 6: SPIKY

The stems of the exotic flowers were **SPIKY**.

P	R	I	C	K	L	Y	H
D	D	E	G	G	A	J	Y
T	E	A	D	E	A	L	B
H	S	G	R	I	T	S	A
O	G	P	N	S	R	H	R
R	B	U	I	O	Y	A	B
N	P	R	O	N	R	R	E
Y	B	S	D	R	Y	P	D

BARBED   ROUGH
BRISTLY   SHARP
JAGGED   SPINY
PRICKLY   THORNY
PRONGED

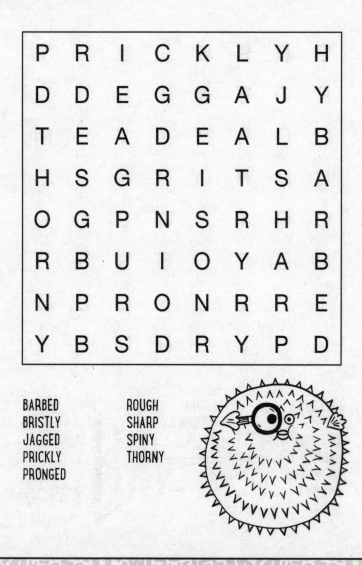

PUZZLE 7: PLACE

She really liked being in this **PLACE**.

```
T  O  P  S  E  O  N  N
I  T  S  U  U  A  O  S
E  S  N  A  S  I  I  E
A  E  R  P  T  G  T  T
V  E  A  A  O  I  I  T
A  C  C  E  S  S  S  I
E  O  N  I  I  C  O  N
L  O  C  A  L  E  P  G
```

AREA
LOCALE
LOCATION
POSITION
SETTING
SITE

SPACE
SPOT
VENUE

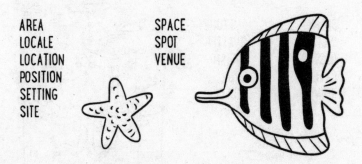

TIME ....

PUZZLE 8: DAMAGE

If you drop that plate, you might **DAMAGE** it.

```
R  U  I  N  O  K  K  F
U  Y  S  U  C  C  R  R
P  R  O  A  E  A  E  S
T  K  R  R  C  T  M  P
U  C  W  T  T  A  A  O
R  C  U  A  S  S  E  I
E  R  H  H  E  A  E  L
E  S  B  R  E  A  K  D
```

BREAK
CRACK
DESTROY
FRACTURE
RUIN

RUPTURE
SHATTER
SMASH
SPOIL
WRECK

PUZZLE 9: MOUNTAIN

It took a long time to climb the **MOUNTAIN**.

```
A  I  M  O  U  N  T  E
T  O  R  O  I  C  L  C
A  S  R  A  R  C  L  H
P  U  M  A  A  I  P  E
E  M  G  N  F  L  L  I
A  M  N  F  A  L  E  G
K  I  S  A  I  I  P  H
P  T  E  H  M  P  O  T
```

ALP   MOUNT
CLIFF   PEAK
CRAG   PINNACLE
HEIGHT   SUMMIT
HILL   TOR

PUZZLE 10: RUN

To catch up with my friend, I had to RUN.

```
R  T  N  I  R  P  S  E
H  E  E  T  B  E  S  T
Y  U  P  G  H  O  U  R
R  E  R  M  R  S  L  O
R  C  T  R  A  A  U  T
U  A  U  N  Y  C  H  R
C  R  H  S  A  D  S  C
S  J  O  G  O  H  E  E
```

BOLT
CHARGE
DASH
HURRY
JOG
RACE
RUSH

SCAMPER
SCURRY
SPRINT
TROT

PUZZLE 11: LAUGH

My friend told me a joke that made me LAUGH.

```
C  H  O  R  T  L  E  C
C  R  E  A  S  E  U  P
G  H  U  T  O  O  H  T
U  G  U  F  F  A  W  I
R  E  K  C  I  N  S  T
A  C  A  C  K  L  E  T
O  G  I  G  G  L  E  E
R  S  N  I  G  G  E  R
```

CACKLE
CHORTLE
CHUCKLE
CREASE UP
GIGGLE
GUFFAW

HOOT
ROAR
SNICKER
SNIGGER
TITTER

PUZZLE 12: CALENDAR

I like to note down important dates on my CALENDAR.

N	T	L	E	E	R	I	E	U	T
S	D	I	A	R	Y	D	P	S	R
J	C	T	M	L	U	L	I	L	S
O	E	H	E	E	A	L	H	T	E
U	Y	H	E	N	T	A	I	T	A
R	M	D	N	D	D	A	R	E	A
N	M	E	L	N	U	A	B	U	R
A	R	E	E	H	H	L	U	L	O
L	E	G	E	C	I	B	E	I	E
A	A	U	L	L	G	G	N	E	D

AGENDA
CHART
DIARY
JOURNAL
LIST
PLANNER
SCHEDULE
TIMETABLE

PUZZLE 13: FAST

The journey into town is always **FAST**.

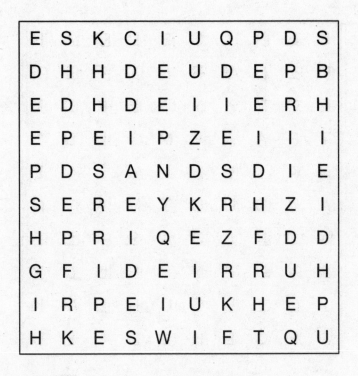

```
E S K C I U Q P D S
D H H D E U D E P B
E D H D E I I E R H
E P E I P Z E I I I
P D S A N D S D I E
S E R E Y K R H Z I
H P R I Q E Z F D D
G F I D E I R R U H
I R P E I U K H E P
H K E S W I F T Q U
```

BRISK
FRENZIED
HIGH-SPEED
HURRIED
QUICK
RAPID
SPEEDY
SWIFT

PUZZLE 14: NEED

If I go shopping, is there anything you **NEED**?

```
L  E  R  I  S  E  D  Q  A  R
K  E  E  S  R  E  N  E  E  E
E  C  V  K  N  T  E  K  D  E
T  R  A  A  E  M  I  E  D  S
N  A  I  L  H  L  K  E  C  E
A  U  D  U  D  T  M  A  V  N
W  C  K  L  Q  A  S  A  E  E
A  V  U  E  N  E  R  U  D  R
I  O  E  D  O  C  R  E  M  K
W  E  C  E  H  L  D  E  E  D
```

CRAVE
DEMAND
DESIRE
LACK
MUST HAVE

REQUIRE
WANT
WOULD LIKE

PUZZLE 15: CORRECT

The winning quiz team gave all **CORRECT** answers.

```
P  E  R  F  E  C  T  L  E  S
F  V  T  G  L  R  H  T  U  S
L  A  U  R  T  O  A  R  R  E
V  T  U  U  R  E  I  F  L
A  N  R  L  U  T  G  A  U  W
L  O  O  C  T  H  H  T  E  A
I  A  C  T  T  L  U  F  E  L
D  A  L  U  O  A  E  U  U  F
L  T  U  V  R  P  R  S  A  L
L  U  F  L  N  T  S  R  S  S
```

ACCURATE   SPOT-ON
FAULTLESS   TRUE
FLAWLESS   TRUTHFUL
PERFECT   VALID
RIGHT

PUZZLE 16: USE

These tools are easy to USE.

```
W  M  E  Z  I  L  I  T  U  E
E  O  N  W  T  K  E  E  T  L
M  U  R  P  I  T  N  A  P  D
T  A  P  K  A  E  L  P  L  N
A  L  N  R  W  U  L  O  P  A
P  A  E  A  P  I  M  D  I  H
E  P  L  I  G  T  T  A  P  L
O  R  N  Y  L  E  L  H  Y  U
E  A  T  Y  O  L  P  M  E  A
M  A  P  P  L  Y  O  L  R  P
```

APPLY
EMPLOY
HANDLE
MANAGE
MANIPULATE

OPERATE
UTILIZE
WIELD
WORK WITH

PUZZLE 17: CHOSEN

My grandmother has a cupboard for her **CHOSEN** teapots.

N	S	E	L	E	C	T	E	D	D
S	U	P	I	D	T	R	E	E	T
U	D	M	E	T	D	R	H	M	R
O	D	E	B	C	R	S	E	E	E
I	E	E	A	E	I	R	F	E	A
C	E	D	F	R	R	A	S	T	S
E	I	E	E	O	E	O	L	S	U
R	R	H	N	E	R	S	N	E	R
P	C	L	A	L	E	C	T	E	E
E	M	O	S	T	L	I	K	E	D

CHERISHED PRECIOUS
DEAREST PREFERRED
ESTEEMED SELECTED
MOST-LIKED SPECIAL
NUMBER-ONE TREASURED

PUZZLE 18: MONSTER

Once upon a time, there was a terrifying **MONSTER**.

```
N T B L N R M R O U
N V D E T O S A E R
T C D V H B M E H T
O R F I T E G E F L
T E E A T L M I D L
E A T T A S E O L H
R T U H E N A O T A
G U R A D R R E T H
O R B N D T D A B E
T E N O G A R D L L
```

BEAST
BEHEMOTH
BRUTE
CREATURE
DEMON

DRAGON
FIEND
LEVIATHAN
OGRE
TROLL

PUZZLE 19: TIRED

After climbing the mountain, everyone felt **TIRED**.

```
L  E  S  S  P  E  T  E  D  R
S  C  X  L  P  F  U  R  E  T
D  H  I  H  E  E  P  A  N  U
Y  E  A  G  A  E  N  E  I  O
S  T  U  T  R  U  P  T  A  N
W  Y  O  G  T  A  S  Y  R  R
O  R  T  U  I  E  H  T  D  O
R  A  A  D  Y  T  R  T  E  W
D  E  G  H  E  H  A  E  E  D
R  W  T  E  E  E  D  F  D  L
```

DRAINED
DROWSY
EXHAUSTED
FATIGUED
LETHARGIC

SHATTERED
SLEEPY
SPENT
WEARY
WORN OUT

PUZZLE 20: QUIET

The deserted beach was always QUIET.

```
N  L  P  E  A  C  E  F  U  L
M  O  I  C  L  S  L  S  S  Y
D  S  I  S  I  E  I  E  D  F
E  M  T  S  D  L  D  T  S  F
H  H  S  I  E  E  L  E  O  S
S  I  L  N  L  L  T  Y  S  L
U  S  T  D  M  L  E  U  D  U
H  M  L  A  C  L  T  S  M  I
S  S  E  L  D  N  U  O  S  S
S  E  H  E  N  E  R  E  S  I
```

CALM   NOISELESS   SOUNDLESS
HUSHED   PEACEFUL   STILL
IDYLLIC   SERENE
MUTED   SILENT

PUZZLE 21: CRY

The wicked witch made the children CRY.

```
I   A   R   S   W   E   E   P   B   E
I   H   O   R   I   W   L   L   R   E
L   B   W   U   E   L   W   E   L   H
L   W   E   D   E   P   B   N   W   W
I   D   O   V   W   B   M   N   A   P
A   H   I   H   U   N   U   I   B   W
W   N   E   L   V   A   H   E   H   E
S   E   B   W   A   I   B   L   W   W
W   S   H   E   D   T   E   A   R   S
E   N   I   H   W   L   P   O   S   E
```

BAWL   SOB
BLUBBER   WAIL
HOWL   WEEP
SHED TEARS   WHIMPER
SNIVEL   WHINE

PUZZLE 22: FIND

Dinosaur fossils can be hard to **FIND**.

```
C  N  T  R  A  C  E  E  D  R
T  O  S  L  A  S  O  N  E  I
O  P  M  R  A  A  T  V  T  R
P  U  U  E  T  E  O  N  E  P
S  N  N  H  A  C  V  L  C  U
C  E  U  E  S  C  O  E  T  G
D  P  T  I  A  C  R  U  R  I
E  P  D  A  A  R  V  O  E  D
A  A  C  T  C  D  T  U  S  L
I  H  E  H  S  P  A  H  E  S
```

COME ACROSS	HAPPEN UPON	TRACE
DETECT	LOCATE	UNEARTH
DIG UP	REVEAL	
DISCOVER	SPOT	

PUZZLE 23: DISAPPEAR

Once the curtains finally opened, the actress felt her worries **DISAPPEAR**.

E	Y	A	W	A	E	I	D	A	E
D	I	E	V	A	E	L	E	V	V
I	M	Y	A	A	A	D	L	P	A
S	E	N	A	S	I	O	A	V	P
S	L	P	P	W	S	T	A	F	O
I	T	W	W	S	A	N	O	N	R
P	A	B	I	A	I	B	W	L	A
A	W	D	E	S	N	A	B	S	T
T	A	F	H	T	A	E	E	E	E
E	Y	R	E	C	E	D	E	A	E

DIE AWAY
DISSIPATE
DISSOLVE
EBB AWAY
EVAPORATE
FADE
LEAVE
MELT AWAY

RECEDE
VANISH
WANE

PUZZLE 24: GUARD

The police were outside a building they needed to **GUARD**.

```
L  E  S  I  V  R  E  P  U  S
V  P  I  C  T  V  E  V  P  S
E  N  O  C  E  V  O  P  A  L
R  E  H  L  R  E  E  R  T  S
B  I  S  E  I  D  V  O  R  H
N  B  S  R  N  C  H  T  O  I
D  B  T  E  E  C  E  E  L  E
O  N  F  S  T  V  S  C  U  L
R  E  I  A  L  E  O  T  R  D
D  R  W  M  E  R  U  C  E  S
```

DEFEND
MIND
OBSERVE
OVERSEE
PATROL
POLICE

PROTECT
SECURE
SHIELD
SUPERVISE
WATCH

INTERMEDIATE

PUZZLE 25: BREATHE

It's so quiet at night that I can hear my dog **BREATHE**.

H	E	P	P	S	N	O	R	T	T
E	T	A	E	G	P	A	T	P	E
F	N	A	R	P	I	U	T	U	R
T	H	P	E	N	U	E	N	E	E
E	E	L	H	R	L	F	S	W	F
Z	L	A	S	A	B	P	F	P	P
E	L	S	H	N	I	W	R	L	S
E	E	X	W	R	O	O	A	T	A
H	E	A	E	F	N	R	E	R	G
W	E	L	H	U	F	F	E	F	D

DRAW BREATH   PUFF
EXHALE   RESPIRE
GASP   SNORE
HUFF   SNORT
INHALE   WHEEZE
PANT

PUZZLE 26: IDEA

After some research, the professor had a new **IDEA**.

```
S  T  H  O  U  G  H  T  P  B
I  U  Y  R  O  E  H  T  R  R
S  A  G  L  I  N  N  O  O  A
E  N  E  G  H  W  P  V  P  I
H  I  O  E  E  I  I  O  O  N
T  S  R  T  N  S  S  T  S  W
O  V  A  I  I  W  T  O  A  A
P  T  O  O  A  O  E  I  L  V
Y  N  N  G  R  U  N  I  O  E
H  T  P  E  C  N  O  C  V  N
```

BRAINWAVE
CONCEPT
HYPOTHESIS
NOTION
OPINION
PROPOSAL

SUGGESTION
THEORY
THOUGHT
VIEW
VISION

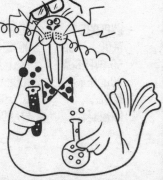

PUZZLE 27: TRAVEL

Adventurers love to **TRAVEL**.

```
P  G  O  T  M  V  E  O  E  S
I  G  E  V  O  R  T  A  A  I
R  T  L  Y  W  R  O  E  E  E
T  V  A  O  E  A  S  A  L  X
A  G  W  M  B  R  N  B  M  P
E  W  L  L  E  E  M  D  E  L
K  E  L  V  M  A  T  O  E  O
A  R  O  R  R  E  G  R  V  R
T  O  K  T  O  U  R  R  O  E
G  Y  E  N  R  U  O  J  B  T
```

EXPLORE
GLOBE-TROT
GO OVERSEAS
JOURNEY
MOVE
RAMBLE

ROAM
ROVE
TAKE A TRIP
TOUR
VOYAGE
WANDER

PUZZLE 28: STORY

The old book contained an unusual STORY.

```
T  E  R  E  P  O  R  T  E  E
N  C  V  E  L  A  T  T  P  E
U  P  A  I  A  E  O  I  L  T
O  P  P  G  T  D  C  C  O  E
C  Y  A  A  C  A  I  E  E  N
C  S  M  E  R  N  R  L  C  R
A  O  N  Y  O  A  B  R  E  A
H  A  R  R  T  A  B  D  A  Y
R  S  H  D  F  H  E  L  R  N
T  C  D  N  E  G  E  L  E  S
```

ACCOUNT
ANECDOTE
CHRONICLE
EPIC
FABLE
LEGEND
MYTH

NARRATIVE
PARABLE
REPORT
SAGA
TALE
YARN

PUZZLE 29: GROUP

The students had gathered outside the school in a large GROUP.

A	O	S	C	T	N	A	Y	Y	G
K	A	Q	R	O	U	A	L	A	R
C	I	U	E	A	H	B	T	A	T
A	B	A	W	C	M	H	M	R	C
P	H	D	N	E	E	G	O	L	C
O	O	U	S	R	N	H	U	R	L
D	B	S	I	A	O	S	O	O	O
N	A	N	G	C	T	W	T	T	M
A	G	H	W	E	D	M	A	E	T
B	T	T	R	M	T	R	O	O	P

ASSEMBLY
BAND
BUNCH
CLUSTER
COHORT
CREW
CROWD

GANG
GATHERING
PACK
SQUAD
TEAM
TROOP

PUZZLE 30: CARRY

The heavy suitcases were tricky to **CARRY**.

```
R  T  R  O  P  S  N  A  R  T
T  F  I  H  S  T  E  R  R  B
R  F  S  H  L  C  A  E  E  Y
V  E  A  U  A  A  D  A  E  A
L  N  V  R  P  L  R  V  E  L
L  U  T  I  U  P  N  N  V  E
U  L  G  O  L  O  O  E  O  R
A  B  H  N  C  E  E  R  M  R
H  S  A  R  L  F  D  L  T  P
U  A  R  E  F  S  N  A  R  T
```

BEAR
CART
CONVEY
DELIVER
HAUL
LUG
MOVE

RELAY
SHIFT
SHOULDER
SUPPORT
TRANSFER
TRANSPORT

PUZZLE 31: KEEP

I use a scrapbook for tickets and souvenirs I wish to **KEEP**.

```
A  C  C  U  M  U  L  A  T  E
O  E  M  A  I  N  T  A  I  N
P  T  V  M  R  C  O  E  S  H
R  C  N  R  H  E  T  N  M  O
E  E  S  O  E  O  T  M  E  L
S  L  S  T  G  S  A  A  E  D
E  L  A  E  O  N  N  R  I  O
R  O  M  O  V  R  A  O  D  N
V  C  A  O  O  A  E  H  C  T
E  P  O  S  S  E  S  S  S  O
```

ACCUMULATE
AMASS
COLLECT
CONSERVE
HANG ON TO
HOARD
HOLD ON TO

MAINTAIN
POSSESS
PRESERVE
RETAIN
SAVE
STORE

PUZZLE 32: SLOWLY

The river flowed very **SLOWLY**.

```
U  I  D  S  I  L  E  B  N  Y  N  D
Y  N  R  E  I  U  A  R  U  Y  E  S
Y  H  H  H  E  E  R  R  L  L  L  S
H  L  E  U  I  D  L  U  I  S  L  L
U  Y  L  T  R  Y  G  B  S  U  R  E
Y  L  G  A  L  R  E  S  G  G  E  I
R  A  L  I  U  R  I  G  Y  Y  L  S
I  R  Z  L  A  D  I  E  R  R  E  U
A  A  G  T  L  S  A  L  D  A  E  R
L  L  E  A  H  U  L  R  I  L  I  E
T  L  S  L  S  Y  U  A  G  Y  Y  L
Y  G  Y  E  A  H  R  L  L  B  U  Y
```

DELIBERATELY
GRADUALLY
LAZILY
LEISURELY
SLUGGISHLY
UNHURRIEDLY

PUZZLE 33: LIE

They told the teacher a LIE.

```
O  L  B  N  N  F  N  C  F  N  D  H
R  A  A  I  A  Y  U  C  F  O  I  T
E  U  P  F  W  T  T  T  O  I  A  U
P  F  N  H  F  U  T  H  E  T  N  R
P  B  I  T  U  W  E  F  O  A  O  T
O  I  B  B  R  S  O  L  H  C  A  F
H  T  T  S  L  U  D  I  R  I  U  L
W  B  F  A  L  T  T  L  A  R  O  A
L  H  F  N  U  A  O  H  I  B  H  H
O  E  Y  R  O  T  S  L  L  A  T  H
T  I  T  T  B  F  N  O  L  F  F  R
T  O  D  T  O  P  A  H  N  S  N  R
```

FABRICATION
FALSEHOOD
FIB
HALF-TRUTH
TALL STORY
UNTRUTH
WHOPPER

PUZZLE 34: DISTANT

The cabin took ages to reach because it was so DISTANT.

```
O  U  E  D  F  A  E  I  E  I  A  L
U  E  L  D  E  C  W  A  C  R  R  T
T  F  B  E  F  D  T  A  W  D  I  N
O  R  I  T  G  A  U  I  O  I  I  C
F  N  S  A  N  L  R  L  F  C  A  O
T  R  S  L  L  S  F  A  C  D  D  U
H  S  E  O  N  I  R  E  W  E  T  E
E  L  C  S  A  F  N  Y  T  A  S  C
W  F  C  I  L  R  S  G  E  M  Y  O
A  D  A  U  T  N  E  T  O  M  E  R
Y  H  N  Y  E  C  L  E  E  S  S  O
A  G  I  S  Y  A  Y  Y  T  R  O  E
```

FAR AWAY   OUT OF THE WAY
FAR-FLUNG   REMOTE
INACCESSIBLE   SECLUDED
ISOLATED

PUZZLE 35: REPLY

After reading a grumpy note from my brother, I decided to **REPLY**.

```
E  R  T  W  N  K  L  A  O  R  R  I
T  R  L  C  T  D  A  T  W  E  S  T
C  R  L  E  R  C  R  N  C  W  I  R
A  E  E  A  T  E  W  I  S  W  B  D
E  A  R  T  S  S  P  S  R  W  R  E
R  S  T  P  A  R  O  I  A  E  E  T
B  O  O  T  O  L  T  P  T  C  A  R
E  N  A  C  E  E  I  O  I  E  O  O
D  E  A  T  B  P  R  A  E  R  C  R
C  T  R  A  A  T  N  I  T  O  R  A
E  E  C  T  R  E  A  R  I  E  R  O
W  K  S  I  W  R  E  T  I  A  C  E
```

ANSWER   RETALIATE
REACT   RETORT
RECIPROCATE   RIPOSTE
RESPOND   WRITE BACK

PUZZLE 36: ENOUGH

The amount of food the chef made was **ENOUGH**.

A	E	S	P	A	S	S	A	B	L	E	S
L	E	A	U	E	U	T	S	A	I	A	A
U	L	L	A	F	B	A	E	T	T	L	T
F	T	E	B	A	F	L	O	I	L	T	E
I	A	E	L	A	E	I	S	S	U	F	L
T	E	R	T	B	N	F	C	L	E	U	P
N	R	T	E	A	A	O	E	I	S	I	M
E	F	E	U	C	U	R	S	F	E	C	A
L	Y	A	T	D	A	Q	E	A	C	N	N
P	E	O	A	F	O	F	E	L	E	E	T
B	R	Y	A	B	F	O	O	D	O	R	S
Y	F	S	O	S	B	C	L	A	A	T	I

ADEQUATE
AMPLE
PASSABLE
PLENTIFUL
REASONABLE
SATISFACTORY

SUFFICIENT
TOLERABLE

PUZZLE 37: POPULAR

The award-winning actor was **POPULAR**.

S	C	A	I	I	D	O	L	I	Z	E	D
C	D	A	E	A	C	T	D	D	R	S	R
E	D	E	M	I	A	L	C	C	A	E	T
L	L	A	D	M	I	R	E	D	T	C	W
E	E	F	D	E	E	L	I	F	S	E	D
B	A	I	E	E	F	N	A	N	L	A	D
R	D	G	D	E	D	T	C	L	D	E	S
A	M	N	A	E	H	N	K	O	D	D	U
T	I	E	M	G	E	N	C	E	O	O	O
E	N	A	U	U	O	Z	K	E	A	E	M
D	N	O	D	W	E	I	N	N	N	E	A
D	S	D	N	U	L	I	R	A	O	B	F

ACCLAIMED
ADMIRED
CELEBRATED
FAMOUS
IDOLIZED
IN DEMAND

LIKED
SOUGHT AFTER
WELL KNOWN

PUZZLE 38: REAL

The art gallery confirmed that the masterpiece was **REAL**.

```
L A D E E E O B V R E E
A E I E D E N G E L T A
I E T I D I A I V L E B
C V B A B E F I U N I F
I N A U M D I A I N A T
F E D L U I H F N I E A
F I T L I D T F I O N G
O T T B M D A I G R B I
E I L G E E O N G I E E
F I C R E D I B L E D V
L A U T H E N T I C L E
I N D I S P U T A B L E
```

AUTHENTIC   LEGITIMATE
BONA FIDE   OFFICIAL
CREDIBLE   VALID
GENUINE   VERIFIED
INDISPUTABLE

PUZZLE 39: DOOR

To solve the maze, they looked for a hidden DOOR.

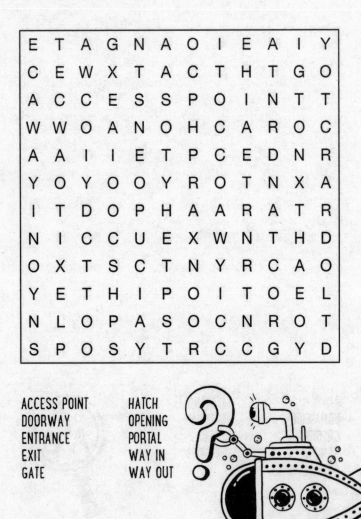

```
E T A G N A O I E A I Y
C E W X T A C T H T G O
A C C E S S P O I N T T
W W O A N O H C A R O C
A A I I E T P C E D N R
Y O Y O O Y R O T N X A
I T D O P H A A R A T R
N I C C U E X W N T H D
O X T S C T N Y R C A O
Y E T H I P O I T O E L
N L O P A S O C N R O T
S P O S Y T R C C G Y D
```

ACCESS POINT   HATCH
DOORWAY   OPENING
ENTRANCE   PORTAL
EXIT   WAY IN
GATE   WAY OUT

PUZZLE 40: WET

After a walk in the rain, all my clothes were **WET**.

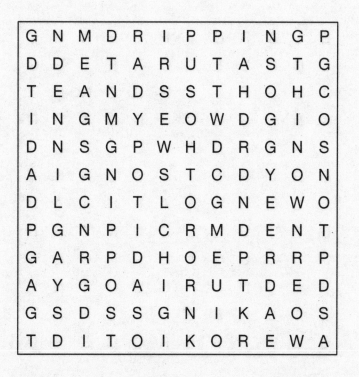

```
G N M D R I P P I N G P
D D E T A R U T A S T G
T E A N D S S T H O H C
I N G M Y E O W D G I O
D N S G P W H D R G N S
A I G N O S T C D Y O N
D L C I T L O G N E W O
P G N P I C R M D E N T
G A R P D H O E P R R P
A Y G O A I R U T D E D
G S D S S G N I K A O S
T D I T O I K O R E W A
```

DAMP
DRENCHED
DRIPPING
MOIST
SATURATED
SOAKING

SODDEN
SOGGY
SOPPING
WATERLOGGED

PUZZLE 41: STRONG

Walls made of stone are very **STRONG**.

```
E U D R G Y E E L H B C
L D O O L O D N F L U G
I U E R L T R R S R N E
T R F S E G S D U I U R
I A S R D S U U T T U R
U B O R E I I S B A S Y
L L L R W W A L D O A D
G E I B R L O L I S R R
R U D G G A E P I E U A
H L S N U H G U O T N H
E I O R S E O R L U R T
L L W R S E R U C E S U
```

DURABLE	ROBUST
HARDY	SECURE
LONG-LASTING	SOLID
POWERFUL	STURDY
RESILIENT	TOUGH

PUZZLE 42: NICE

The new swimming teacher was very **NICE**.

```
P  L  E  A  S  A  N  T  H  O  Y  D
L  D  F  L  O  V  E  L  Y  E  E  N
D  D  S  T  I  E  C  G  L  R  Y  G
E  N  W  L  S  G  N  G  U  L  N  A
L  G  E  L  P  K  L  T  D  I  G  G
I  M  E  O  Y  S  A  N  M  E  C  R
G  T  T  N  A  N  E  R  N  K  L  E
H  R  R  P  D  I  A  I  I  R  N  E
T  Y  L  O  R  H  A  N  V  N  G  A
F  L  O  F  C  L  D  E  A  G  F  B
U  G  L  A  T  D  A  E  E  U  R  L
L  T  A  G  L  R  R  U  L  T  C  E
```

AGREEABLE   LOVELY
CHARMING   PLEASANT
DELIGHTFUL   SWEET
FRIENDLY
GENIAL
GOOD-NATURED
KIND

PUZZLE 43: BEAUTIFUL

This painting is **BEAUTIFUL**.

```
A  G  T  I  T  T  O  E  T  N  V  R
F  O  G  N  I  N  N  U  T  S  E  A
G  O  I  E  O  N  G  T  T  T  T  D
Y  D  E  S  I  R  G  R  I  T  L  E
T  L  X  V  I  O  I  S  R  O  S  L
T  O  C  R  S  K  I  A  V  U  Y  I
E  O  O  L  I  U  C  E  O  N  D  G
R  K  X  N  Q  T  L  E  O  Y  O  H
P  I  G  X  I  Y  G  G  T  S  T  T
G  N  E  V  S  R  E  L  K  S  R  F
H  G  E  T  O  I  T  D  L  R  O  U
R  G  I  G  T  N  A  I  D  A  R  L
```

ATTRACTIVE   LOVELY
DELIGHTFUL   PRETTY
EXQUISITE   RADIANT
GOOD-LOOKING   STRIKING
GORGEOUS   STUNNING

PUZZLE 44: PROBABLY

Whenever you hear birdsong at night, it is **PROBABLY** nearly dawn.

```
A  C  U  S  T  O  M  A  R  I  L  Y
R  S  N  A  N  U  I  R  D  M  O  L
Y  T  A  R  M  K  I  O  Y  O  Y  Y
Y  L  T  R  D  C  U  L  U  S  M  L
L  U  I  Y  U  B  L  S  S  T  U  L
E  I  N  R  T  L  U  S  U  O  S  A
O  O  K  L  A  A  E  A  E  F  B  C
N  A  E  E  L  N  C  T  T  T  S  I
R  S  D  L  L  L  I  I  S  E  U  P
S  O  Y  E  T  Y  Y  D  L  N  Y  Y
N  O  R  M  A  L  L  Y  R  L  T  T
K  E  G  A  R  E  V  A  N  O  S  A
```

AS A RULE   MOST OFTEN   TYPICALLY
CUSTOMARILY   NORMALLY   USUALLY
DOUBTLESS   ON AVERAGE
LIKELY   ORDINARILY

⏱ TIME ....

PUZZLE 45: SMALL

The toy was particularly SMALL.

```
I  I  C  C  O  M  P  A  C  T  E  E
M  T  E  E  Y  E  Y  L  T  E  P  L
E  I  E  R  M  E  P  P  E  M  E  U
V  S  C  E  U  I  N  O  C  I  L  C
I  N  E  R  N  T  T  I  R  N  T  S
M  E  E  L  O  Y  A  E  A  U  T  U
T  U  T  M  Y  S  I  I  M  T  I  N
E  I  O  I  T  N  C  T  N  E  L  I
V  P  L  E  T  M  I  O  U  I  I  M
M  I  P  U  M  E  M  T  P  N  M  I
E  U  O  P  M  E  P  E  L  I  L  C
D  I  M  I  N  U  T  I  V  E  C  I
```

COMPACT
DIMINUTIVE
LITTLE
MICROSCOPIC
MINIATURE

MINUSCULE
MINUTE
PETITE
TEENY
TINY

PUZZLE 46: SEPARATE (ADJECTIVE)

The two buildings appeared connected but were actually entirely **SEPARATE**.

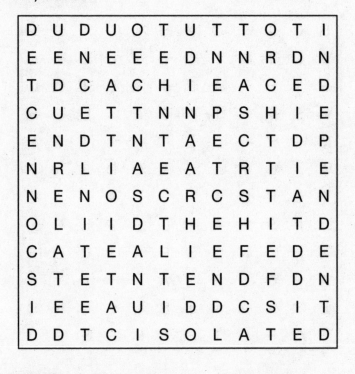

```
D U D U O T U T T O T I
E E N E E E D N N R D N
T D C A C H I E A C E D
C U E T T N N P S H I E
E N D T N T A E C T D P
N R L I A E A T R T I E
N E N O S C R C S T A N
O L I I D T H E H I T D
C A T E A L I E F E D E
S T E T N T E N D F D N
I E E A U I D D C S I T
D D T C I S O L A T E D
```

APART　　　　DISTANCED　　　UNATTACHED
DETACHED　　　DISTINCT　　　　UNRELATED
DIFFERENT　　　INDEPENDENT
DISCONNECTED　ISOLATED

PUZZLE 47: LEARN

Foreign languages can be difficult to **LEARN**.

```
S  G  A  I  C  P  U  K  C  I  P  G
S  U  T  H  T  G  E  S  U  E  E  C
S  Y  U  R  A  R  I  A  S  T  A  O
K  B  M  N  I  A  E  E  T  U  S  M
M  G  E  U  D  E  T  H  C  T  G  P
A  A  Q  O  E  E  E  O  D  R  N  R
T  C  B  D  T  H  R  O  A  I  T  E
A  Y  S  S  A  P  G  S  E  U  R  H
N  H  D  N  O  S  P  K  T  Q  O  E
A  R  G  U  E  R  A  N  T  A  Y  N
E  O  K  G  T  T  B  U  C  O  N  D
F  O  R  E  T  S  A  M  R  E  B  D
```

ABSORB
ACQUIRE
COMPREHEND
GET THE HANG OF
GRASP
MASTER

PICK UP
STUDY
TAKE IN
UNDERSTAND

PUZZLE 48: OLD

The furniture in the museum was **OLD**.

```
O  C  I  R  O  T  S  I  H  E  R  P
S  L  N  D  G  T  A  L  R  I  A  H
D  C  D  D  E  R  N  D  E  S  A  D
G  E  D  F  C  D  S  E  T  C  E  D
I  T  T  H  A  G  O  I  I  T  I  A
N  D  A  A  E  S  T  M  A  C  I  C
I  I  R  M  U  S  H  D  T  C  N  N
C  A  L  A  P  Q  T  I  L  U  A  A
G  R  S  R  D  I  I  H  O  O  O  T
A  R  I  I  E  T  E  T  D  N  D  E
E  M  I  A  G  A  G  E  N  Q  E  O
E  H  E  G  A  T  N  I  V  A  C  D
```

AGED
ANCIENT
ANTIQUATED
ARCHAIC
DATED

OLD-FASHIONED
OUTMODED
PAST ITS PRIME
PREHISTORIC
VINTAGE

PUZZLE 49: PROJECT

I've started work on a new **PROJECT**.

```
E  E  E  R  U  T  N  E  V  T  G  M
S  S  S  I  N  A  L  P  I  N  T  E
S  P  M  C  A  A  S  E  I  E  I  S
Y  A  N  H  H  I  N  K  M  M  V  I
P  T  O  M  M  E  A  C  T  N  P  R
E  M  I  E  I  T  M  A  A  G  I  P
R  V  J  V  R  S  I  E  E  I  R  R
O  O  O  E  I  S  S  P  I  S  N  E
B  T  D  T  N  T  B  I  E  S  E  T
E  N  S  E  G  A  C  E  O  A  I  N
U  I  R  K  S  A  T  A  E  N  I  E
N  E  X  E  R  C  I  S  E  I  T  B
```

ACTIVITY
ASSIGNMENT
ENTERPRISE
EXERCISE
JOB
MISSION

PLAN
SCHEME
TASK
UNDERTAKING
VENTURE

PUZZLE 50: WANT

Winning the competition is all that we **WANT**.

E	R	Y	P	R	A	Y	F	O	R	P	C
R	H	E	O	R	O	E	F	W	E	R	R
A	O	R	T	T	A	F	A	N	A	S	R
E	P	L	R	F	E	N	H	V	O	T	R
E	E	I	O	D	A	R	E	S	F	A	F
C	F	Y	R	N	E	R	I	P	I	R	O
A	O	F	C	H	G	S	E	P	F	W	A
A	R	F	A	O	R	F	I	K	S	P	P
R	H	E	F	H	R	O	O	R	N	A	S
W	R	O	F	E	N	I	P	R	E	A	P
I	F	F	R	F	O	M	A	E	R	D	H
A	F	D	A	R	O	F	N	R	A	E	Y

ASPIRE TO
CRAVE
DESIRE
DREAM OF
HANKER AFTER
HOPE FOR

LONG FOR
PINE FOR
PRAY FOR
WISH FOR
YEARN FOR

PUZZLE 51: CONFRONT

I wanted to know where my brother had hidden my shoes, so I decided to **CONFRONT** him.

```
Z E L L I R G R E L E C
W U T E E S G I R T R Q
E O T A C K L E A O G U
I R T A I A Z G S A E E
V E E S A I O S E G I S
R S O K U R E T N C Y T
E O M Q R X A E L R N I
T L C E A E L C E A T O
N G T M A L C U C N G N
I N I L A R Q C C O T X
I N I H I K T O U K S Q
E L C X C U R R V E A T
```

ACCOST
ASK
CHALLENGE
CROSS-EXAMINE
GRILL
INTERROGATE
INTERVIEW

QUERY
QUESTION
QUIZ
TACKLE

PUZZLE 52: FRIEND

I had a good chat with my **FRIEND**.

N	A	L	E	D	A	R	M	O	C	E	L
E	C	N	A	T	N	I	A	U	Q	C	A
C	C	L	I	E	N	F	F	I	S	B	E
C	F	A	O	T	I	C	B	I	K	I	I
O	C	P	C	N	N	T	D	M	A	N	B
M	I	U	F	A	N	E	S	C	C	U	U
P	L	F	N	D	K	C	I	E	D	I	D
A	B	N	N	I	Y	C	U	D	B	B	I
N	Q	A	C	F	O	L	Y	C	H	U	M
I	U	K	C	N	C	A	L	A	L	S	A
O	N	T	D	O	C	D	U	A	I	P	Q
N	Y	O	M	C	T	I	M	Q	K	A	I

ACQUAINTANCE   CONFIDANT
ALLY   PAL
BESTIE   SIDEKICK
BFF
BUDDY
CHUM
COMPANION
COMRADE

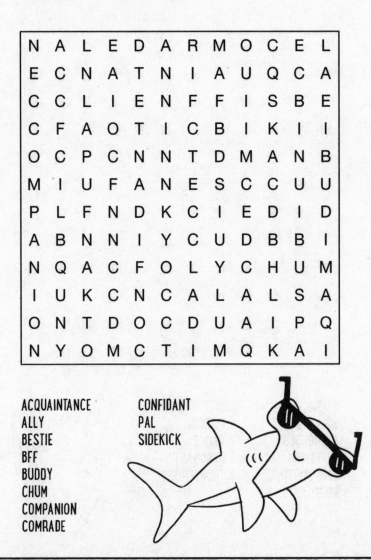

PUZZLE 53: LOUD

The noise from the music festival was LOUD.

```
E  N  C  S  B  D  O  E  D  T  N  O
N  A  M  L  S  L  A  L  H  E  D  V
A  U  R  N  A  U  A  U  L  E  A  E
U  S  N  S  N  M  N  R  A  R  P  R
W  R  U  O  P  D  O  F  I  I  G  W
N  S  I  O  E  L  E  R  E  N  D  H
O  S  E  R  C  N  I  R  O  U  G  E
Y  C  O  N  I  U  C  T  R  U  T  L
T  U  S  N  C  I  A  G  T  O  S  M
S  G  G  O  N  O  O  R  L  I  H  I
E  A  S  G  N  I  M  O  O  B  N  N
L  R  E  S  O  N  A  N  T  A  L  G
```

BLARING	OVERWHELMING
BOOMING	PIERCING
CLAMOROUS	RAUCOUS
DEAFENING	RESONANT
EAR-SPLITTING	THUNDEROUS
NOISY	

PUZZLE 54: LOTS

On a woodland walk, we saw LOTS of fallen leaves.

S	P	I	S	P	I	L	E	S	E	E	L
E	S	S	A	E	S	T	D	H	S	O	P
N	M	I	K	U	R	E	L	E	S	O	L
P	R	A	H	C	R	O	O	A	S	C	S
L	I	S	S	D	A	O	C	P	E	H	T
E	U	S	N	S	S	T	D	S	L	O	O
N	O	U	L	O	E	A	S	E	D	S	N
T	H	S	E	O	I	S	S	S	O	N	S
Y	T	L	D	S	A	L	K	I	O	Y	S
S	M	S	N	N	P	D	L	R	A	I	N
D	K	L	S	N	U	D	S	I	S	N	D
A	N	S	S	D	N	U	O	M	M	S	L

HEAPS
HUNDREDS
LOADS
MASSES
MILLIONS
MOUNDS
OODLES

PILES
PLENTY
SCORES
STACKS
TONS

PUZZLE 55: SEPARATE (VERB)

To take apart the model, there will be lots of pieces to **SEPARATE**.

```
O T T S L T N O E D N F
X D D C L E N A I V T F
I I N J E H V S N P I O
F S N U C N M O U N T K
N O C A N A N T M K O A
U D T U N C I O A E S E
F E O T R L O N C N R R
D U L A P X F U B S O B
P E T S N O U N P G I A
N A N I O J S I D L L D
D I S E N T A N G L E O
U F F O T U C O O A A N
```

BREAK OFF   DISENTANGLE   SPLIT UP
CUT OFF   DISJOIN   UNCOUPLE
DETACH   DISMANTLE   UNDO
DISCONNECT   REMOVE   UNFIX

PUZZLE 56: PARTY

For the Queen's birthday, the King organized a great **PARTY**.

H	B	A	N	Q	U	E	T	A	J	B	R
C	E	L	E	B	R	A	T	I	O	N	E
L	E	U	A	A	O	S	B	L	A	G	H
F	N	S	U	E	A	A	E	J	N	G	T
E	T	T	E	E	S	E	I	I	C	L	E
T	E	N	F	H	L	E	R	A	R	A	G
E	F	F	A	I	N	E	R	A	N	V	O
I	U	L	B	E	H	N	T	E	R	I	T
B	A	U	H	T	I	S	E	I	O	T	T
G	J	T	A	V	E	N	R	A	T	S	E
I	H	G	A	I	E	L	S	R	E	E	G
E	A	L	F	S	N	E	B	T	E	F	V

BANQUET
BASH
CARNIVAL
CELEBRATION
FEAST
FESTIVAL
FETE

FIESTA
GALA
GATHERING
GET-TOGETHER
JUBILEE

PUZZLE 57: RECALL

Happy memories are easy to **RECALL**.

```
D T T C E V O K E W I E
R N B C O C E U T E E L
E W I R E N L K I I E D
T R T M I L J G C V R N
R R T I O N L U E E E I
I L E R C T G O R R T K
E S E M V I G B C E E E
V U O I E E L N A E U R
E M O I E M R E I C R P
U M E V E D B R E R K L
B O K V I O C E B M B O
R N U I C E V R R R I I
```

BRING BACK
BRING TO MIND
CONJURE UP
ELICIT
EVOKE
RECITE
RECOLLECT

REKINDLE
REMEMBER
RETRIEVE
REVIEW
SUMMON

PUZZLE 58: SHOUT

To get her attention, I had to **SHOUT**.

```
I  K  L  L  H  S  R  O  C  M  A  M
A  R  L  O  R  E  L  L  O  H  A  S
S  A  R  K  E  T  A  L  L  E  C  E
W  B  A  E  R  N  C  L  R  K  O  H
M  E  O  I  L  A  W  C  W  L  C  M
R  R  R  R  L  R  S  O  L  S  S  W
E  E  Y  H  R  H  A  E  L  S  O  L
Y  C  E  S  R  O  L  O  A  L  W  E
E  R  S  C  L  L  R  R  L  O  E  O
E  O  C  L  B  H  L  L  H  E  M  B
B  R  A  O  E  E  E  A  L  S  M  L
E  C  I  O  V  Y  M  E  S  I  A  R
```

BARK
BELLOW
CALL
CRY
HOLLER
HOWL
RAISE MY VOICE
RANT

ROAR
SCREAM
SHRIEK
YELL

TIME ....

PUZZLE 59: WATCH

Tomorrow night there is a meteor shower that I want to **WATCH**.

```
Z T K S T A R E A T R E
S A T R S M A B V V E A
C A T C H S I G H T O F
Z A S H E V R E S B O A
T L S A E N I D S A R Y
A G U R M N I G C T I A
K S R E S O A M A A R E
O S V P W Z N R A A F O
O E E M E E E I G X C S
L C Y A R E I R T P E P
T R T K P I T V O O E G
O D D R A G E R R R R L
```

CATCH SIGHT OF
EXAMINE
GAZE AT
INSPECT
LOOK AT
MONITOR
OBSERVE
PEER AT

REGARD
STARE AT
SURVEY
VIEW

PUZZLE 60: SAY

I could not hear what the man tried to **SAY**.

```
R  U  E  M  E  T  R  T  T  G  E  H
E  S  I  E  E  E  C  S  R  I  I  O
P  S  R  N  T  E  R  O  H  E  S  M
S  O  G  T  A  T  A  E  R  O  U  T
I  Y  C  I  T  N  X  H  L  R  U  S
H  R  A  O  S  C  X  L  M  C  S  T
W  C  O  N  L  X  E  U  O  E  E  S
L  M  U  A  I  Y  R  A  R  X  L  M
U  T  I  T  T  H  E  P  S  N  H  I
U  M  E  U  T  N  X  I  H  I  M  U
U  S  L  M  E  E  G  T  S  S  N  E
L  R  T  E  O  H  R  S  L  X  O  I
```

CRY
EXCLAIM
EXPRESS
GROAN
HISS
MENTION
MURMUR
SHOUT

SIGH
STATE
UTTER
WHISPER
YELL

PUZZLE 61: BUILD

The inventor liked to **BUILD** things.

A	H	E	O	M	D	R	C	E	R	F	A
C	R	E	A	T	E	O	M	F	A	S	G
D	N	K	I	P	M	O	A	S	S	O	E
E	E	U	A	P	C	B	H	E	N	E	C
V	I	H	O	C	R	I	M	O	S	C	U
I	S	S	R	I	O	B	N	S	B	A	D
S	E	E	C	N	L	A	E	I	H	E	O
E	C	A	I	E	H	S	F	E	I	M	R
S	T	N	G	I	S	E	D	S	A	R	P
E	C	O	N	S	T	R	U	C	T	O	E
U	E	M	O	F	R	O	R	C	L	F	A
C	E	R	U	T	C	A	F	U	N	A	M

ASSEMBLE   FASHION
COMPOSE   FORM
CONSTRUCT   MAKE
CREATE   MANUFACTURE
DESIGN   PRODUCE
DEVISE   SHAPE
FABRICATE

PUZZLE 62: SEE

The camouflaged snow leopard was hard to SEE.

```
D I S T I N G U I S H I
E B C P E N W E I V O D
R P I I E Y S D R E T N
I S N P G S E I V E R R
E O S B E N P R N E E T
N E S S T R E M C T I U
R O V I E S C O I N V O
E I F V B N G E O L V E
C Y I O I N T T I S G K
S R C I I M I I P V R A
I S E Z I C T Y W O E M
D N E T E E C S P O T P
```

DISCERN
DISTINGUISH
GLIMPSE
IDENTIFY
MAKE OUT
NOTICE
OBSERVE

PERCEIVE
RECOGNIZE
SPOT
SPY
VIEW
WITNESS

PUZZLE 63: BRAVE

To face your fears you must be **BRAVE**.

```
T  O  G  A  I  N  T  R  E  P  I  D
L  T  N  A  L  L  A  G  R  Y  H  G
T  I  D  E  T  E  R  M  I  N  E  D
Y  C  O  U  R  A  G  E  O  U  S  F
G  K  D  N  N  G  N  U  V  G  E  D
U  K  C  D  H  C  G  A  C  A  F  L
T  L  C  U  I  E  L  N  R  N  S  O
S  L  N  O  L  I  A  L  I  E  T  B
Y  L  R  S  A  P  E  R  L  R  U  H
A  E  A  N  S  S  N  R  T  L  A  S
H  S  T  E  S  R  H  F  E  E  L  D
D  A  U  N  T  L  E  S  S  G  D  P
```

BOLD
COURAGEOUS
DARING
DAUNTLESS
DETERMINED
FEARLESS
GALLANT

GUTSY
HEROIC
INTREPID
LION-HEARTED
PLUCKY
VALIANT

PUZZLE 64: TIDY

The sailor made sure his cabin was always TIDY.

```
S S E S Y L R E D R O D
S P R H S G Y C E M E E
H R I S L P E C O R L I
I I H C E D H R E B M H
P S E A K S G T A M E S
S T R M E A T T A I S T
H I O R N U N C R E M H
A N F I L E U D L A I E
P E Z C S L I T S E M N
E E N E A L O E F P A S
D U R T R P T A E N A N
U P E P S S P S L E K N
```

CLEAN
FRESH
IMMACULATE
NEAT
ORDERLY
ORGANIZED
PRESENTABLE

PRISTINE
SHIPSHAPE
SMART
SPICK AND SPAN
SPOTLESS
UNCLUTTERED

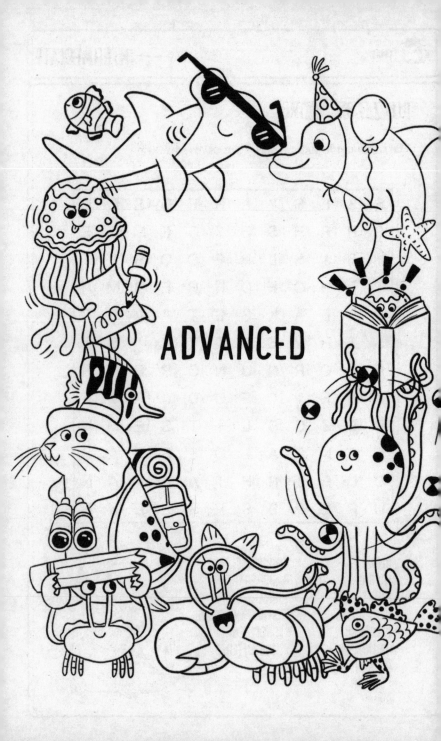

ADVANCED

PUZZLE 65: WEIRD

Being abducted by aliens would be extremely **WEIRD**.

```
G  S  N  Y  D  D  F  I  N  O  R  E
N  U  N  D  M  S  L  O  R  L  L  G
I  R  O  M  O  S  M  B  A  B  N  G
X  R  F  Y  X  M  I  M  A  I  I  U
E  E  A  P  O  Z  R  C  Y  R  S  N
L  A  K  C  A  O  I  F  R  T  Y  U
P  L  N  R  N  L  I  E  R  N  K  S
R  U  R  B  P  T  G  A  L  R  A  U
E  E  A  X  S  U  N  I  M  E  E  A
P  N  E  Y  L  G  D  E  U  L  R  L
I  N  M  A  E  K  L  E  L  U  F  F
I  S  R  T  R  A  I  L  U  C  E  P
```

ABNORMAL
BIZARRE
FREAKY
INEXPLICABLE
IRREGULAR
MYSTIFYING
ODD
PECULIAR

PERPLEXING
STRANGE
SURREAL
UNCOMMON
UNUSUAL

PUZZLE 66: COLD

During our snowy walk, the air outside felt COLD.

Y	R	C	F	L	L	W	I	I	C	H	Z
R	I	R	F	O	Z	A	A	O	A	L	C
T	C	E	C	A	S	F	O	R	A	I	G
N	Y	T	I	E	C	L	S	G	F	F	G
I	I	T	T	L	R	H	N	R	R	L	G
W	A	I	C	I	G	I	E	F	A	A	N
Y	E	B	R	W	Z	S	R	C	I	O	I
A	L	I	A	E	H	O	I	H	O	I	C
I	H	L	E	R	S	A	I	Y	S	N	R
H	T	R	I	T	L	Y	P	P	I	N	E
P	F	O	Y	H	P	I	A	R	G	Y	I
C	R	I	L	Y	C	E	I	C	I	A	P

ARCTIC
BITTER
CHILLY
COOL
FREEZING
FRESH
FROSTY

GLACIAL
HARSH
ICY
NIPPY
PIERCING
RAW
WINTRY

PUZZLE 67: STORM

We found a safe place to shelter from the **STORM**.

I	T	H	U	N	D	E	R	G	C	H	H
T	P	A	N	T	N	T	N	H	U	U	T
O	H	T	N	D	S	I	D	N	R	N	O
R	A	T	M	E	N	R	C	R	T	D	R
R	I	H	P	T	A	Y	I	N	N	U	N
E	L	M	H	Z	C	C	N	I	O	H	A
N	E	G	Z	L	A	O	W	P	W	D	D
T	I	I	O	N	O	L	N	R	A	N	O
L	L	N	E	S	R	W	L	S	O	I	R
B	E	R	N	I	O	L	L	A	U	Q	S
I	O	O	H	D	R	H	T	Y	U	R	L
N	M	W	U	W	R	T	G	A	L	E	H

BLIZZARD MONSOON
CYCLONE SQUALL
DOWNPOUR TEMPEST
GALE THUNDER
HAIL TORNADO
HURRICANE TORRENT
LIGHTNING WHIRLWIND

PUZZLE 68: HOT

On our family holiday, the weather was HOT.

```
L  G  N  I  R  A  E  S  M  R  A  W
Y  A  N  S  G  F  I  M  G  S  W  I
T  A  R  R  C  Z  I  N  R  A  A  G
S  S  A  L  Z  A  I  E  G  I  N  N
A  S  C  L  A  T  L  F  R  I  L  B
O  F  I  O  S  C  R  D  R  Y  B  S
T  N  B  A  R  G  I  E  I  O  E  U
G  O  O  A  N  C  T  P  I  N  N  M
T  R  C  I  L  L  H  L  O  L  G  M
T  L  K  R  E  M  I  I  M  R  G  E
I  A  M  W  N  N  Y  A  N  A  T  R
B  Z  S  S  G  T  R  L  R  G  S  Y
```

BAKING	SEARING
BALMY	SIZZLING
BOILING	SUMMERY
FIERY	SWELTERING
ROASTING	TOASTY
SCALDING	TROPICAL
SCORCHING	WARM

PUZZLE 69: BIG

The dinosaur skeleton at the museum was **BIG**.

```
M  M  H  U  M  O  N  G  O  U  S  G
E  U  O  I  S  A  M  M  L  G  S  E
L  E  A  U  A  U  A  L  A  A  G  T
B  T  V  A  N  M  O  R  A  U  L  A
A  S  E  I  M  T  G  M  H  R  I  A
Z  A  N  O  S  A  A  G  R  A  G  N
I  V  T  I  N  S  N  I  I  O  N  E
S  H  T  T  E  V  A  N  N  A  N  S
U  S  U  A  O  S  M  M  L  O  N  E
N  A  C  I  T  N  A  G  I  G  U  T
N  S  N  I  M  M  E  N  S  E  I  S
I  S  U  B  S  T  A  N  T  I  A  L
```

ENORMOUS
GARGANTUAN
GIANT
GIGANTIC
HUGE
HUMONGOUS
IMMENSE

LARGE
MAMMOTH
MASSIVE
MOUNTAINOUS
SIZABLE
SUBSTANTIAL
VAST

PUZZLE 70: SCARY

I heard a ghost story that I found **SCARY**.

E	G	N	I	Y	F	I	R	T	E	P	N
T	G	N	I	L	L	I	H	C	D	E	F
E	I	R	E	E	N	N	Y	A	R	R	O
R	R	E	R	N	I	K	U	V	I	G	R
R	S	N	O	E	O	N	E	G	N	E	B
I	H	O	G	O	T	R	H	I	T	C	I
F	O	I	P	I	A	T	M	S	R	R	D
Y	C	S	N	C	E	R	I	E	I	R	D
I	K	G	K	N	A	N	E	I	N	K	I
N	I	I	I	L	I	P	N	N	V	I	N
G	N	N	A	S	Y	A	R	N	O	C	G
G	G	N	I	S	I	A	R	R	I	A	H

ALARMING
CHILLING
CREEPY
DAUNTING
EERIE
FORBIDDING
FRIGHTENING

HAIR-RAISING
NERVE-RACKING
PETRIFYING
SHOCKING
SINISTER

SPOOKY
TERRIFYING

PUZZLE 71: WALKED

Did you see which way they **WALKED**?

```
S  T  E  P  P  E  D  E  D  U  H  E
D  G  K  C  C  E  R  E  O  I  W  S
R  A  E  T  L  R  T  D  S  K  D  T
D  E  D  W  S  M  E  A  C  A  E  R
R  E  A  J  O  T  U  P  W  L  K  A
D  R  H  V  O  N  R  D  T  J  K  I
C  A  E  S  T  G  L  O  R  D  E  P
S  D  K  E  A  E  G  H  L  A  R  S
A  S  R  P  D  D  H  E  I  L  T  E
D  E  H  C  R  A  M  C  D  K  E  D
D  L  D  D  E  L  B  M  A  E  E  D
S  D  S  K  I  P  P  E  D  L  E  D
```

AMBLED
CRAWLED
CREPT
DASHED
DAWDLED
HIKED
JOGGED
MARCHED

MOVED
SAUNTERED
SKIPPED
STEPPED
STROLLED
TRAIPSED
TREKKED

PUZZLE 72: SAD

When her friend moved away, the girl felt SAD.

```
N  M  O  S  O  R  R  O  W  F  U  L
D  E  V  A  S  T  A  T  E  D  D  E
M  L  L  D  E  J  E  C  T  E  D  D
I  A  G  L  M  M  M  P  T  R  E  L
S  N  L  N  A  U  U  R  U  S  I  Y
E  C  O  A  L  F  A  M  S  D  P  D
R  H  O  G  M  E  T  E  G  P  E  U
A  O  M  F  H  S  R  S  A  A  P  F
B  L  Y  N  H  T  I  H  E  S  D  U
L  Y  W  E  S  O  N  D  E  R  S  E
E  O  E  I  R  U  A  T  O  R  C  E
D  D  D  M  D  O  L  E  F  U  L  S
```

CRESTFALLEN	FED UP	UNHAPPY
DEJECTED	GLOOMY	UPSET
DEVASTATED	GLUM	
DISMAL	MELANCHOLY	
DISTRESSED	MISERABLE	
DOLEFUL	SORROWFUL	
DOWNHEARTED		

PUZZLE 73: THINK

After the talk, the professor began to **THINK**.

```
R T D C M U S E M R M T
C E U E O E O T T E E U
A O V O L G E O O F D O
E C N O T I I A U L I T
T C A T T I B T K E T I
A P O L E I E E A C A K
L O U N C M L L R T T R
U N E D S U P L Z A E O
C D Z N E I L L U Z T W
E E I O M M D A A M U E
P R E D N O W E T T U P
S E T A N I M U R E E M
```

CALCULATE
COGITATE
CONSIDER
CONTEMPLATE
DELIBERATE
MEDITATE
MULL IT OVER
MUSE

PONDER
PUZZLE IT OUT
REFLECT
RUMINATE
SPECULATE
WONDER
WORK IT OUT

PUZZLE 74: IMPORTANT

The doctors explained why their work was **IMPORTANT**.

```
Y M E A N I N G F U L Y
H T P A R A M O U N T L
T R N R V O T T A I C A
R C V A R A N H R I R I
O S R T C E L O I E U T
W U A I I I I U L E C N
E V R L T R F E A V I E
T V A G P I V I I B A S
O S Y H E A C T N L L S
N S G E N N A A A G A E
L I C T K L T R L M I C
H A Y R A S S E C E N S
```

CRITICAL
CRUCIAL
ESSENTIAL
HIGH PRIORITY
KEY
MEANINGFUL
NECESSARY
NOTEWORTHY

PARAMOUNT
RELEVANT
SALIENT
SIGNIFICANT
URGENT
VALUABLE
VITAL

PUZZLE 75: BAD

The evil queen's treatment of the princess was **BAD**.

```
D T S A G P N A E T L G
A E S U A N W A H I A P
T R S E O F I O S L T G
R R R P U D R G U T N A
O I E L I R N F A I Y H
C B A L I C D E L M O R
I L T B I A A L R R A E
O E L N E V A B R R L D
U E E R N P B I L S O R
S B D L P E D I R E I H
E L B A T P E C C A N U
I T N A S A E L P N U G
```

APPALLING
ATROCIOUS
AWFUL
DAMAGING
DESPICABLE
DIRE
DREADFUL
HORRENDOUS

HORRIBLE
HORRID
NASTY
TERRIBLE
UNACCEPTABLE
UNPLEASANT
VILE

PUZZLE 76: HAPPY

Playing with balloons makes me feel **HAPPY**.

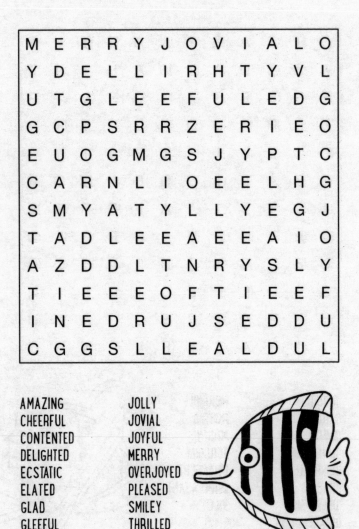

```
M  E  R  R  Y  J  O  V  I  A  L  O
Y  D  E  L  L  I  R  H  T  Y  V  L
U  T  G  L  E  E  F  U  L  E  D  G
G  C  P  S  R  R  Z  E  R  I  E  O
E  U  O  G  M  G  S  J  Y  P  T  C
C  A  R  N  L  I  O  E  E  L  H  G
S  M  Y  A  T  Y  L  L  Y  E  G  J
T  A  D  L  E  E  A  E  E  A  I  O
A  Z  D  D  L  T  N  R  Y  S  L  Y
T  I  E  E  E  O  F  T  I  E  E  F
I  N  E  D  R  U  J  S  E  D  D  U
C  G  G  S  L  L  E  A  L  D  U  L
```

AMAZING	JOLLY
CHEERFUL	JOVIAL
CONTENTED	JOYFUL
DELIGHTED	MERRY
ECSTATIC	OVERJOYED
ELATED	PLEASED
GLAD	SMILEY
GLEEFUL	THRILLED

PUZZLE 77: TAKE

Unattended bags are easy for thieves to TAKE.

```
C  B  C  A  P  T  U  R  E  U  F  R
A  C  C  T  P  U  K  C  I  P  C  Q
E  G  O  S  L  P  N  E  F  A  A  P
Z  R  R  N  S  E  R  O  R  U  U  O
I  A  S  A  F  U  R  R  A  R  E  P
E  B  R  E  C  I  Y  I  L  F  L  I
S  G  C  O  C  O  S  O  U  A  C  N
R  N  R  N  F  U  I  C  E  Q  P  C
R  P  E  F  U  N  R  T  A  U  C  H
S  N  A  T  C  H  S  E  N  T  L  A
H  G  E  T  H  O  L  D  O  F  E  R
A  C  E  G  Q  N  I  A  T  B  O  B
```

ACQUIRE
CAPTURE
CARRY OFF
CONFISCATE
GET HOLD OF
GRAB
GRASP
OBTAIN

PICK UP
PINCH
PROCURE
PURLOIN
SECURE
SEIZE
SNATCH
STEAL

PUZZLE 78: GREAT

I love my friends because they are GREAT.

M	C	I	F	I	R	R	E	T	A	E	L
G	A	T	W	A	U	C	M	N	S	L	F
N	C	G	O	G	A	F	O	E	T	B	I
I	I	S	N	N	A	F	S	L	O	A	R
D	T	P	D	I	A	G	E	L	N	K	S
N	S	L	E	L	F	N	W	E	I	R	T
A	A	E	R	Z	S	I	A	C	S	A	C
T	T	N	F	Z	U	Z	C	X	H	M	L
S	N	D	U	A	P	A	L	E	I	E	A
T	A	I	L	D	E	M	A	R	N	R	S
U	F	D	U	G	R	A	I	Z	G	T	S
O	S	U	O	L	L	E	V	R	A	M	G

ACE
AMAZING
ASTONISHING
AWESOME
DAZZLING
EXCELLENT
FANTASTIC
FIRST CLASS

MAGNIFICENT
MARVELLOUS
OUTSTANDING
REMARKABLE
SPLENDID
SUPER
TERRIFIC
WONDERFUL

PUZZLE 79: DIFFICULT

The last puzzle was extremely **DIFFICULT**.

E	C	E	E	K	N	O	T	T	Y	T	C
Y	D	L	U	M	A	H	H	O	U	O	O
G	E	E	E	G	O	R	A	R	S	U	M
N	S	X	T	M	N	S	D	R	N	G	P
I	U	U	H	A	O	I	I	U	D	H	L
D	O	T	O	A	C	S	L	R	O	X	E
N	U	R	I	I	U	I	E	F	A	U	X
A	N	I	R	R	R	S	L	R	F	E	S
M	E	C	U	E	I	O	T	P	I	A	W
E	R	K	O	R	A	N	B	I	M	T	B
D	T	Y	Y	M	I	E	G	A	N	O	U
S	S	O	B	S	C	U	R	E	L	G	C

ARDUOUS   LABORIOUS
BAFFLING   OBSCURE
COMPLEX   STRENUOUS
COMPLICATED   TIRESOME
DEMANDING   TIRING
EXHAUSTING   TOUGH
HARD   TRICKY
KNOTTY   WEARISOME

PUZZLE 80: HELP

They were struggling, so I decided to **HELP**.

```
M E G A E A D N A B D D M D E
M O A I U T E I N E M E O H P
E P E O V T A C P O H L I D D
H I E D I A P R H T E E I A G
T L E L S O D P E I T A E A I
E I D T I M C G B P E H D L D
D A D A A A A M D D O H P E L
I E E R R R O M I D I O D N R
U U G E U I O V C T S U C D T
G E C O A A O B A S L A E A T
T E C N E R D U A U O A A H D
S N C I P T M L R L O O H A E
E E E O H T A E I O L D D N M
N R A S S I S T H S O O D D S
A M E H T T R O P P U S C A E
```

ASSIST
COLLABORATE
CO-OPERATE
ENCOURAGE THEM
GUIDE THEM
LEND A HAND
PROVIDE AID
SUPPORT THEM

PUZZLE 81: SLEEP

After a big lunch, I like to **SLEEP**.

```
Z E F O O F F O T F I R D F R
I H G D F O T B L V S F T N Y
G E H Y Z D I S D F S D F A A
R E A I A F F R E I O O F T R
E E T O R A A A R R M T O R A
B O I F T P Z N E O S E D E N
M E B U O D E A N S O S O S N
U E E B S R B T E I T E N H I
L D R S F T T E A R T E F B R
S D E H O L O Y R N Z D E E N
V O Z O N P I F W O R S I F A
P Z O E A E W S O I R E M D A
A E R N S F I N S O N T B B O
U O N S A R S I O E O K R I L
H A V E A S I E S T A S S S H
```

DOZE
DRIFT OFF
GET FORTY WINKS
HAVE A SIESTA
HIBERNATE
NAP
NOD OFF

REST
SLUMBER
SNOOZE

TIME ....

PUZZLE 82: APPEAR

After reading the spooky story, I wondered if a ghost might **APPEAR**.

```
A R H M R E C T I W U R E I F
V M L E Z F S N O T E L G R L
L A N I R E E M I E B V E P E
E A S O F S E I B I E S S U S
C E T I R V F C S A M R A W T
P I N I I V R I C A S N E O I
I A E R P P V A T R F I U H T
M R R S U E I E M E A E I S N
R A E N M I R E E C P M I E E
G B R O F I S U R F A C E N S
T U C B A E E O P S I E T S E
T E E L C P P C B U N A B S R
B O I L F U V O I T E O I P P
F Z O N P E N C E C T E L O S
E E M E R G E R E F L E A S A
```

ARRIVE
BECOME VISIBLE
CROP UP
EMERGE
ENTER
MANIFEST

MATERIALIZE
PRESENT ITSELF
SHOW UP
SURFACE
TURN UP

PUZZLE 83: REGAL

The royal family looked very **REGAL**.

I	I	U	A	Q	U	E	E	N	L	Y	E	G	S	U
Y	E	N	D	N	A	R	G	M	I	N	T	P	I	N
G	E	N	I	O	M	Y	L	I	E	K	E	E	G	S
L	A	C	I	H	C	R	A	N	O	M	S	Y	A	M
I	L	D	E	H	S	I	U	G	N	I	T	S	I	D
S	U	A	A	A	C	T	Y	L	E	C	N	I	R	P
A	S	B	I	Y	L	I	A	R	G	G	D	T	N	L
A	B	E	C	R	M	S	M	T	I	Y	G	S	E	U
Y	R	R	I	I	E	A	U	P	E	I	A	M	T	G
C	N	L	R	I	T	P	J	K	O	L	C	S	D	C
S	K	O	Q	E	E	E	M	E	I	S	Y	S	I	C
N	N	A	B	J	D	R	M	I	S	N	I	G	I	I
A	M	L	P	L	I	N	T	E	N	T	G	N	Y	L
I	S	U	G	B	E	I	N	R	T	E	I	L	G	A
I	C	G	M	E	Y	S	R	M	G	N	E	C	Y	O

DISTINGUISHED
GRAND
IMPERIAL
IMPOSING
KINGLY
MAJESTIC

MONARCHICAL
NOBLE
PRINCELY
QUEENLY
STATELY

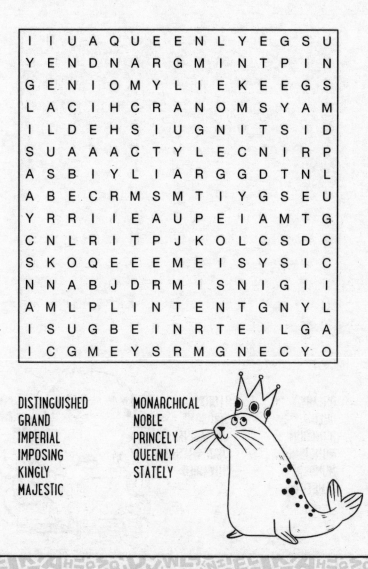

PUZZLE 84: BORING

I thought the TV show was really **BORING**.

```
S  O  U  D  A  G  N  D  R  E  A  R  Y  N  I
N  U  U  I  E  R  E  T  E  D  I  O  U  S  G
T  S  O  N  M  E  U  A  T  N  A  T  I  M  U
I  I  U  N  I  N  T  E  R  E  S  T  I  N  G
M  R  R  U  O  M  I  N  Y  E  U  U  R  T  Y
D  M  E  E  A  T  A  U  I  D  U  E  V  N  M
E  U  E  P  S  O  O  G  R  S  I  I  P  V  T
I  N  I  M  E  O  R  N  I  N  M  V  T  I  E
R  D  U  D  H  T  M  T  O  N  R  T  V  N  T
A  A  V  E  N  R  I  E  A  M  A  E  N  D  E
V  N  E  U  Y  M  N  T  G  O  T  T  U  O  V
N  E  D  T  L  E  N  L  I  E  O  I  I  I  Y
U  U  E  L  N  M  M  T  N  V  T  U  U  V  L
I  D  U  A  V  S  S  R  R  M  E  U  E  E  E
T  D  M  U  R  D  M  U  H  D  R  E  O  Y  I
```

DREARY
DULL
HUMDRUM
MONOTONOUS
MUNDANE
REPETITIVE

TEDIOUS
TIRESOME
UNIMAGINATIVE
UNINTERESTING
UNVARIED

PUZZLE 85: ACTIVITY

I enjoyed taking part in this **ACTIVITY**.

```
T M N N P S L R D Y M I T T M
E E S P C I R T S E S S E M I
T R R C O A E P N R U U H G M
T N O E O T O M E E D I O A N
O R E I C R A T I R E S B M O
N T O M T R E T E T M R B E I
C D T D N I E T E N S S Y I T
T I T N E I E A T E I A P O C
U V R T E S A T T I S R P I A
A E E E I M I T E I N S E E R
T R B S H E E C R E O R B E T
C S E Y E E E S R E S N V R S
T I A N A R E T U E T A A C I
E O H R N L M E Y M X N S A D
E N N H A S P T I I A E E U R
```

AMUSEMENT   ENTERTAINMENT   HOBBY   RECREATION
DISTRACTION   EXERCISE   PASTIME   SPORT
DIVERSION   GAME   PLAY

PUZZLE 86: GROW

The plant began to **GROW**.

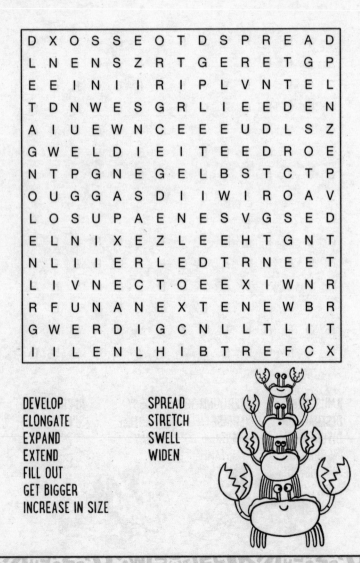

```
D X O S S E O T D S P R E A D
L N E N S Z R T G E R E T G P
E E I N I I R I P L V N T E L
T D N W E S G R L I E E D E N
A I U E W N C E E E U D L S Z
G W E L D I E I T E E D R O E
N T P G N E G E L B S T C T P
O U G G A S D I I W I R O A V
L O S U P A E N E S V G S E D
E L N I X E Z L E E H T G N T
N L I I E R L E D T R N E E T
L I V N E C T O E E X I W N R
R F U N A N E X T E N E W B R
G W E R D I G C N L L T L I T
I I L E N L H I B T R E F C X
```

DEVELOP
ELONGATE
EXPAND
EXTEND
FILL OUT
GET BIGGER
INCREASE IN SIZE

SPREAD
STRETCH
SWELL
WIDEN

PUZZLE 87: NAUGHTY

My puppy is cute but **NAUGHTY**.

```
T D D T R O U B L E S O M E T
D I E R V E R H E N E P E U O
C S V U E E I B E E D L R N I
O O A R N C N N T I B L L D M
A B H B E A A N U A L M S I S
T E E I I B A L E E I N S S S
L D B E Y I E M C S L E A C E
D I Y R F L A L C I H Y S I I
P E L E V T U H L D T L T P A
N N D L N A I R U I E R O L I
R T A U I E L O N I O B A I R
U W B S V U E Y I U O U B N O
D D B O N T F I I R A C S E T
A S U U H D R A W Y A W P D A
E S E L B I G I R R O C N I O
```

BADLY BEHAVED   TROUBLESOME
DEFIANT   UNDISCIPLINED
DISOBEDIENT   UNRULY
INCORRIGIBLE   UNTAMEABLE
MISCHIEVOUS   WAYWARD
REBELLIOUS
RECALCITRANT

PUZZLE 88: BEGIN

The scientists were excited to **BEGIN** their new project.

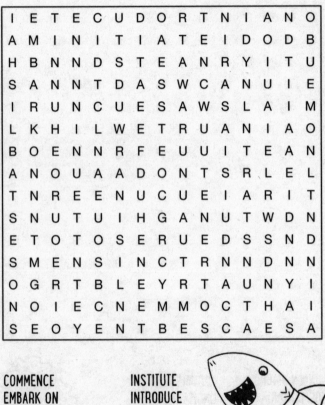

```
I  E  T  E  C  U  D  O  R  T  N  I  A  N  O
A  M  I  N  I  T  I  A  T  E  I  D  O  D  B
H  B  N  N  D  S  T  E  A  N  R  Y  I  T  U
S  A  N  N  T  D  A  S  W  C  A  N  U  I  E
I  R  U  N  C  U  E  S  A  W  S  L  A  I  M
L  K  H  I  L  W  E  T  R  U  A  N  I  A  O
B  O  E  N  N  R  F  E  U  U  I  T  E  A  N
A  N  O  U  A  A  D  O  N  T  S  R  L  E  L
T  N  R  E  E  N  U  C  U  E  I  A  R  I  T
S  N  U  T  U  I  H  G  A  N  U  T  W  D  N
E  T  O  T  O  S  E  R  U  E  D  S  S  N  D
S  M  E  N  S  I  N  C  T  R  N  N  D  N  N
O  G  R  T  B  L  E  Y  R  T  A  U  N  Y  I
N  O  I  E  C  N  E  M  M  O  C  T  H  A  I
S  E  O  Y  E  N  T  B  E  S  C  A  E  S  A
```

COMMENCE

EMBARK ON

ESTABLISH

FOUND

GET UNDER WAY ON

INAUGURATE

INITIATE

INSTITUTE

INTRODUCE

LAUNCH

START

PUZZLE 89: EXCITING

The story in my spy book was **EXCITING**.

A	G	G	G	N	I	T	A	R	A	L	I	H	X	E
C	N	C	I	T	A	M	A	R	D	H	A	E	N	A
T	I	N	B	A	G	N	N	C	T	E	B	T	R	G
I	Y	S	G	R	A	N	N	C	N	M	H	L	N	T
O	F	E	O	N	E	I	I	T	E	R	R	I	T	Y
N	I	N	H	I	I	A	I	U	A	Y	L	G	O	N
P	R	S	L	I	T	L	T	L	G	G	N	N	T	G
A	T	A	G	H	E	L	L	H	N	I	P	R	I	T
C	C	T	H	A	I	I	N	I	T	M	R	A	N	P
K	E	I	E	R	N	X	T	I	R	A	B	T	A	O
E	L	O	I	G	I	E	B	A	I	H	K	T	N	N
D	E	N	F	Y	N	L	R	A	D	A	T	I	A	I
Y	S	A	C	I	I	I	I	E	I	A	A	T	O	N
A	T	L	P	A	Y	K	I	L	F	H	I	R	Y	G
O	R	S	N	S	T	I	M	U	L	A	T	I	N	G

ACTION-PACKED
BREATHTAKING
DRAMATIC
ELECTRIFYING
ENTHRALLING
EXHILARATING

INTRIGUING
NAIL-BITING
SENSATIONAL
SPINE-TINGLING
STIMULATING
THRILLING

PUZZLE 90: ALMOST

The new aquarium building was **ALMOST** finished.

```
Y L L A I T N E S S E A T R L
P Y L T S O M A O V L T E N Y
Y R A N E Y S T I F S R S A L
L L A C O L J R A Y L S N R L
L A T C R T T U L Y E Y B N J
A R O F T U F E S L L A Y I A
T A R A A I G A R T S R N E C
N E E L R R C O R I A L A L E
E U L L A S E A C F T B U E E
M Y C L T R L A L R R U O R N
A A O L O E L T N L Y O T U T
D T A M O L Y T E L Y R M L T
N R O Y Y A O A N L M Y E L C
U A Y N L M E E F M L T L L A
F L U L C L O S E T O A I U Y
```

BASICALLY   MOSTLY
CLOSE TO   NEARLY
ESSENTIALLY   NOT FAR FROM
FUNDAMENTALLY PRACTICALLY
JUST ABOUT   VIRTUALLY
LARGELY
MORE OR LESS

PUZZLE 91: HIDDEN

The spies had to make sure they remained **HIDDEN**.

```
D D D T R E V O C L E L D O I
T E U E S N R E N U R D S I C
C S E S G O A C N R O U R E N
O I U S S A E G I G O O N E C
N U I G A O L U R I D U L U C
C G R L S T Y F T E N O E N L
E S V F A N D I U D D T A D A
A I N T E E T I E O E E C E N
L D C E R P U R F R M U U S D
E E S E E U C S C G C A U H E
D N V R E O C S E N S C C L S
U O R E V O I R F L S E T L T
C U U E I D L F U R T I V E I
S C R N V Y H T L A E T S G N
T F N V S E C R E T E O O A E
```

CAMOUFLAGED
CLANDESTINE
CONCEALED
COVERED
COVERT
DISCRETE
DISGUISED

FURTIVE
SECRET
STEALTHY
SURREPTITIOUS
UNDERCOVER
UNSEEN

PUZZLE 92: CLEVER

The student who won the prize was **CLEVER**.

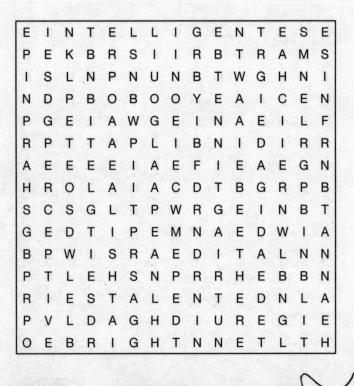

```
E   I   N   T   E   L   L   I   G   E   N   T   E   S   E
P   E   K   B   R   S   I   I   R   B   T   R   A   M   S
I   S   L   N   P   N   U   N   B   T   W   G   H   N   I
N   D   P   B   O   B   O   O   Y   E   A   I   C   E   N
P   G   E   I   A   W   G   E   I   N   A   E   I   L   F
R   P   T   T   A   P   L   I   B   N   I   D   I   R   R
A   E   E   E   E   I   A   E   F   I   E   A   E   G   N
H   R   O   L   A   I   A   C   D   T   B   G   R   P   B
S   C   S   G   L   T   P   W   R   G   E   I   N   B   T
G   E   D   T   I   P   E   M   N   A   E   D   W   I   A
B   P   W   I   S   R   A   E   D   I   T   A   L   N   N
P   T   L   E   H   S   N   P   R   R   H   E   B   B   N
R   I   E   S   T   A   L   E   N   T   E   D   N   L   A
P   V   L   D   A   G   H   D   I   U   R   E   G   I   E
O   E   B   R   I   G   H   T   N   N   E   T   L   T   H
```

ADEPT	KNOWLEDGEABLE
BRAINY	PERCEPTIVE
BRIGHT	SHARP
CAPABLE	SHREWD
GIFTED	SMART
INGENIOUS	TALENTED
INTELLIGENT	

PUZZLE 93: NEW

The designer came up with something **NEW**.

```
O G T P T C E C S Y F T U C R
T E R R I E P T U T U N S T V
R C N O U O R C R R P E R I C
E O E D U N N E O R R A N O T
D F A E R N C E E U E E N O U
R E U E N E D C E H I T N Y F
N O D T N N E B T R E A C T E
E O E T U D O F R M I R E A V
M N R N E R O R P E R N T N R
U N O N T E I O I C A V G C R
U S T V T T R S N G D K O C H
M E G A E A N N T O I E I S D
D R T N R L R E E I T N E N R
R S K Y N N D S R C C R A R G
I N N O V A T I V E F E E L O
```

CONTEMPORARY
CURRENT
FRESH
FUTURISTIC
GROUNDBREAKING
INNOVATIVE
MODERN

NOVEL
ORIGINAL
PIONEERING
RECENT
STATE-OF-THE-ART
UNPRECEDENTED

PUZZLE 94: KIND

When I got lost, the police officer who helped was **KIND**.

```
S Y M P A T H E T I C I A L L
R C R L E S U A N D Y H T N E
N R O G U H G H G L S K O U T
E O U M V F E E D K I A N U D
T P R H P L T N N N D D L H E
A B I C P A E H D E E T M T R
R B E F O I S H G R R N D O U
E O U N R U E S S U B O T S T
D L B F E A R T I A O P U E A
I D T L R V A T M O V H E S N
S D E T I N O I E S N N T O D
N T E H D G A L C O D A U C O
O D O I N B I S E C U L T G O
C I N G L D O N O N F S N E G
N G E E E R T L G O T T H P E
```

AMIABLE
BENEVOLENT
COMPASSIONATE
CONSIDERATE
COURTEOUS
FRIENDLY
GENEROUS
GOOD-NATURED

HELPFUL
KIND-HEARTED
OBLIGING
SYMPATHETIC

THOUGHTFUL
UNDERSTANDING

PUZZLE 95: ORDINARY

Without my friends, life feels so **ORDINARY**.

```
P R E D I C T A B L E L A A D
L N T C G N M D S P V I A E U
E L P M I S E U N P E A H R G
O I I B O H R D R C A S M A T
N E T S E N U D A D I L D V N
B S N S N A V L U U M M O E O
I L N A N T P L G N O U L R R
M C A R D N C U D N R H A M
R I G N O N I C E T U I L G A
N R S M D T U S M H S L U E L
U M M M S N T M S I D U S E G
I O C I I U M I S H E S E I D
C C D A N O N D E S C R I P T
E N L D U L L N M E M N N H C
U P M C O N V E N T I O N A L
```

AVERAGE   MUNDANE
BLAND   NONDESCRIPT
COMMONPLACE   NORMAL
CONVENTIONAL   PLAIN
DULL   PREDICTABLE
HUMDRUM   SIMPLE
MODEST   UNDISTINGUISHED

PUZZLE 96: SURPRISED

When she saw the magic trick, the girl was **SURPRISED**.

```
E F O A E D S H F D B D A F R
S O L D D A E C R A B S D N E
T E O A D R A I S L T E L I V
A D D G B A D T F O Y N T L O
R X D B E B O E U E B A Z Z D
T A N Z L N E N X K P A V O E
L L G D I O D R E O V U E D L
E I E S M E W S G A M N T D W
D F H D D S T N T A L M T S O
H E D D E W O W A U S S U W B
D A M A Z E D S U W N T G L V
F S H O C K E D T S A N E K F
T A K E N A B A C K M Y E D A
T A E D U M B F O U N D E D K
T R N S T A G G E R E D E S F
```

AMAZED
ASTONISHED
ASTOUNDED
BLOWN AWAY
BOWLED OVER
DUMBFOUNDED
FLABBERGASTED
FLUMMOXED

SHOCKED
STAGGERED
STARTLED
STUNNED
STUPEFIED
TAKEN ABACK
WOWED

PUZZLE 97: DIRTY

The floor of the dragon's cave was **DIRTY**.

N	Y	L	Y	H	T	L	I	F	G	L	U	O	F
Y	A	M	N	G	F	N	A	E	L	C	N	U	Y
Y	U	S	Y	T	D	S	M	Y	F	I	V	S	M
F	D	U	L	G	A	U	R	U	F	F	U	T	I
F	I	F	T	N	N	R	S	H	C	I	N	A	L
U	B	E	Y	L	T	I	N	T	U	K	G	I	S
R	Y	G	S	R	R	H	T	I	Y	F	Y	N	S
C	G	R	G	H	F	S	N	S	S	S	Y	E	Q
S	Y	U	N	R	A	G	O	Y	U	H	Y	D	U
H	A	B	G	N	I	B	D	A	E	G	E	R	A
B	C	B	B	U	N	M	B	S	U	L	S	D	L
R	Y	Y	N	Y	Y	T	Y	Y	A	I	I	I	U
U	L	R	S	B	E	T	M	U	U	N	G	V	D
T	U	N	W	A	S	H	E	D	A	N	I	E	E
U	L	R	N	M	K	I	T	N	L	B	W	D	I

DISGUSTING   SCRUFFY   UNWASHED
DUSTY   SHABBY   VILE
FILTHY   SLIMY
FOUL   SQUALID
GRIMY   STAINED
GRUBBY   TARNISHED
GRUNGY   UNCLEAN
MUCKY

⏱ TIME ....

PUZZLE 98: ANNOUNCE

I have something important to **ANNOUNCE**.

```
T  E  D  E  C  L  A  R  E  A  N  N  O  N  N
S  T  R  T  M  H  B  T  E  T  A  T  S  R  S
M  N  L  E  E  T  A  R  R  A  N  L  E  V  E
I  U  G  E  P  M  N  O  O  U  T  T  E  R  S
A  O  R  S  C  O  N  O  S  A  E  I  R  R  T
L  C  N  O  S  T  R  H  I  N  D  E  E  A  A
C  E  L  L  E  E  O  T  W  T  L  C  B  M  E
O  R  E  C  D  W  A  O  T  A  N  T  A  T  E
R  R  D  S  L  L  N  L  T  I  S  E  A  S  A
P  A  E  I  N  K  T  E  S  L  R  E  M  B  T
M  T  A  D  E  R  E  O  E  T  I  C  E  R  E
C  E  E  K  A  O  R  E  V  E  A  L  R  T  E
P  D  A  P  R  E  E  B  I  R  C  S  E  D  N
E  M  M  A  C  U  E  E  G  L  U  V  I  D  E
R  I  S  R  M  S  E  R  L  O  A  I  R  R  D
```

BROADCAST
DECLARE
DESCRIBE
DISCLOSE
DIVULGE
IMPART
MAKE KNOWN
MENTION

NARRATE
PROCLAIM
RECITE
RECOUNT
RELATE
REPORT
REVEAL
SHOW

STATE
UTTER

PUZZLE 99: ANGRY

The man in the broken-down car was **ANGRY**.

```
R E D E S A E L P S I D E R F
D U P I N A R M S R I E P R S
D T A D H O F U R I O U S H N
R E R D E E D E G A R N E O G
I O T D E T A I I X E H P P N
N I U A I T A T I S A R I P I
C G M T R I A I E P R I A I G
E E L G R E R T R D N L N N A
N S U I N A P A I U I E R G R
S X I D V I G S T R F D E M D
E S R E G I G E A E R N U A A
D M A M O O D Y D X T I I D S
R M O E E E O U R I E D A R N
O A E U I G N I H T E E S N E
U D S E E I N G R E D N R I P
```

DISPLEASED   INFURIATED   RILED
ENRAGED   IRATE   SEEING RED
EXASPERATED   IRRITATED   SEETHING
FURIOUS   LIVID   UP IN ARMS
HEATED   MOODY
HOPPING MAD   OUTRAGED
INCENSED   RAGING

PUZZLE 100: ALLOW

She asked permission, but the school did not **ALLOW** it.

```
C A E T A R E L O T E O S Z P A E
E G Z N A I S T N T A E L P T N C
R O A G C O N S E N T T O S F T E
A I T R G R O P E T G A L G R V I
R O F N O I S S I M R E P E V I G
G T O O N U C Z V T V D G E S V E
R E T N A R R A W A T R O R T O I
T E E V O R P P A A E E S U R S R
R A U E O W O N E E F E T S R T A
M L L E E T T T N O Z N A A R N S
I O I L E N O L N I A O P N A E A
I S F E A A I R R E D P M E N T N
O E R R R G R O A E E O T D P E C
P G G T H H H E Z R T M O V E T T
A T R T I T E S M O R R R A S I I
E N E R U N E I E A S G E T R T O
N I A A E O T I P E P T H S R O N
```

AGREE TO
APPROVE
AUTHORIZE
CONSENT TO
ENDORSE
GIVE PERMISSION FOR
GRANT

GREEN-LIGHT
PERMIT
SANCTION
TOLERATE
WARRANT

BONUS
PUZZLES

PUZZLE 101: SHADES OF BLUE

```
A L A I D C Y A N R E I C
M T R C E O A S K Y L U O
I A U D N E H T E A L I R
D D C O I P R L S T N E N
N T N E M C A U R A N P F
I R L C R Y U A Z I R O L
G O M A O U M U R A L W O
H G N R B A L A G N E D W
T L O A R O M E T O E E E
E R E I V A C U A E A R R
H T N T U Y A N I N O Q D
N E T Q S A P P H I R E K
N N A T U R Q U O I S E U
```

AQUAMARINE	POWDER
AZURE	ROYAL
CERULEAN	SAPPHIRE
COBALT	SKY
CORNFLOWER	TEAL
CYAN	TURQUOISE
DENIM	ULTRAMARINE
MIDNIGHT	
NAVY	

PUZZLE 102: SHADES OF RED

```
R L D R D K B R I C K I I
N R U F O R T E B G E B S
Y B A C B E F R R N A U C
Y B N S Y I E B I L T T U
B B I B P R C M B R A C C
T U E E I B R A R G M E R
E E R R D A E E E O T R I
T I L G C T L R H I G I M
S L K R U U A Y R C S S S
E Y C L A N R I Y Y U E O
I L A V A C D F L A M E N
G A R N E T S Y B R R L C
A S R V R I C O T S V E C
```

BRICK
BURGUNDY
CARMINE
CERISE
CHERRY
CRIMSON
FLAME
GARNET
LAVA

RASPBERRY
RUBY
SCARLET

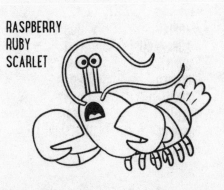

PUZZLE 103: SHADES OF GREEN

```
O A E L E I M A N E J S O
R O R E A V S V R A J D S
T O A A G A I A E R U L T
G B P R S R P L F I N A S
L O S F E P A P O I G R E
I L O N E V A S L E L E R
A B L A R B O R S E E M O
L I S L O R L L A M C E F
R M O T E R A O C G I G L
T S T D M O E P U J U N U
F L L O R M A E P E A S T
E L S S I E A A S T P D B
R S T L G O P R I E E R E
```

APPLE	JUNGLE
ASPARAGUS	LIME
BOTTLE	MINT
CLOVER	MOSS
EMERALD	OLIVE
FERN	PEAR
FOREST	
GRASS	
JADE	

PUZZLE 104: SHADES OF YELLOW

```
C A N A R Y U M R D M L W
M L Z P L O D A E N T N L
U R D N O M L A T O D T I
S S I B E E E Z R L B D D
T P R D C G S I A B Y N O
A L U E L I O O R P R O F
R W M C W N T L R O O B F
D S A E R O O R D M U T A
O R D R L E L M O E I C D
M N A D T S T F E N N R T
T N C O B S T T N L A L P
O U E A N O N E U U D F D
D E G I E B D E R B S G Y
```

ALMOND
BEIGE
BLOND
BUTTERCUP
CANARY
CITRON
DAFFODIL
GOLDEN
LEMON

MUSTARD
PRIMROSE
STRAW
SUNFLOWER
TOPAZ

PUZZLE 105: EMOTIONS

```
I  H  I  R  E  L  I  E  V  E  D  D  P
L  D  A  A  A  F  R  A  I  D  E  R  R
L  O  E  X  C  I  T  E  D  T  G  E  O
U  A  J  T  N  S  N  E  N  U  M  A  U
F  N  E  E  A  E  U  I  A  B  I  S  D
E  G  A  C  R  R  O  O  A  G  U  E  A
P  R  L  V  O  P  T  R  I  R  E  G  G
O  Y  O  L  P  N  R  S  P  X  I  R  U
H  U  U  A  U  A  T  R  U  T  N  Y  I
S  D  S  E  S  F  I  E  A  R  P  A  L
G  I  D  S  B  S  Y  T  N  P  F  P  T
D  A  E  I  E  D  E  O  A  T  S  S  Y
S  D  X  D  S  D  T  H  J  D  F  L  E
```

AFRAID	FRUSTRATED	SAD
AGITATED	GUILTY	SURPRISED
ANGRY	HAPPY	
ANXIOUS	HOPEFUL	
CONTENT	JEALOUS	
DISAPPOINTED	JOYFUL	
EAGER	NERVOUS	
EMBARRASSED	PROUD	
EXCITED	RELIEVED	

PUZZLE 106: THE WATER CYCLE

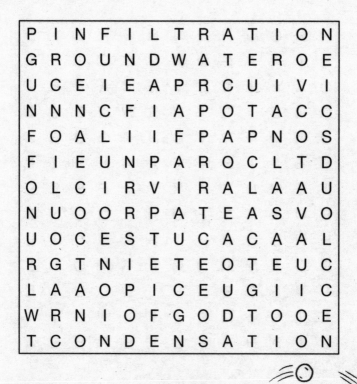

```
P I N F I L T R A T I O N
G R O U N D W A T E R O E
U C E I E A P R C U I V I
N N C F I A P O T A C C
F O A L I I F P A P N O S
F I E U N P A R O C L T D
O L C I R V I R A L A A U
N U O O R P A T E A S V O
U O C E S T U C A C A A L
R G T N I E T E O T E U C
L A A O P I C E U G I I C
W R N I O F G O D T O O E
T C O N D E N S A T I O N
```

CLOUDS
COLLECTION
CONDENSATION
EVAPORATION
GROUNDWATER
INFILTRATION
OCEAN
PRECIPITATION
RAIN

RUN-OFF
TRANSPIRATION
WATER VAPOUR

PUZZLE 107: THE WEATHER

```
H N G T H U N D E R E L D
E I A A G D R Y E C I E R
O A L I N S T E M A R H I
G R E I G I H R W U Z S Z
D N W O D T O H T O U H Z
E E I I S T E A A N H T L
T E M N S A R T S E S S E
R U I H T E O H L O C N S
H H G W P H I E R S L T L
B O A M M N G F T N O O E
F V E C E H E I E O U I E
E T S I M E Z T L W D I T
L I A H A E Z E E R B E A
```

BREEZE	ICE	TEMPERATURE
CLOUD	LIGHTNING	THUNDER
DRIZZLE	MIST	WIND
FOG	RAIN	
FROST	SHOWER	
GALE	SLEET	
HAIL	SNOW	
HEATWAVE	STORM	
HUMIDITY	SUNSHINE	

PUZZLE 108: NATURAL WATER FEATURES

```
Y A A A R D E K A L V O R
O E P P T T D A P T A R N
A S B M P N P A Y A S O E
M N B O O U E R O C O E P
A C O P D L A A A G A R R
R L R D B U E N A A E I K
E V L S T R A L Y P O V E
S E D S O L O T N V O E I
E T E O N S E O R E D R E
I I R A R L E E K I E P I
I A E E N C S T R A L E Y
L C L I A E B S P D T A O
O R E A R M E E L K A T U
```

BROOK
CANAL
DELTA
ESTUARY
INLET
LAGOON
LAKE
OCEAN
POND

POOL
PUDDLE
RESERVOIR
RIVER
SEA
STREAM
TARN

WORD-GROUP SEARCH →   ⏰ TIME ....

PUZZLE 109: STORY SETTINGS

```
N F U T U R I S T I C C I T Y
D E G P U E I D C E R T M T O
H A D K I T E C D E E C E R U
O O E R A H S I S V I L L E T
E C S V A E S E S A P K T S E
I R S U A G P E R O T C S E R
S H U R B C D N T O I S A D S
R C O C O M S E I A F R C Y P
B O S K M T A N T A R N R D A
E S I H T N T R O N T I I N C
A O C P G U E Y I G A N P A E
C G O R N P H A S N A H U S R
H N A N T T I K E Y E R C O H
C A S A I S P R I E E G D N M
E S U O H D E T N U A H R N E
```

BEACH   RAINFOREST
CASTLE   SANDY DESERT
DRAGON'S CAVE   SUBMARINE
ENCHANTED GARDEN
FUTURISTIC CITY
HAUNTED HOUSE
MOUNTAIN PEAK
OUTER SPACE
PIRATE SHIP

PUZZLE 110: TYPES OF BOOK

```
E G S A O K I O O O A T E
E D P R K O O O R N C N Y
U I O O O O R O T R C H R
G C K I E K O H B Y O T A
O T C O N T O B C T H G I
L I N S O L R L E E X A D
A O K O O B O Y S D C E B
T N A G V P K A B I I O T
A A Y H E E U O M O O U Y
C R K D D R L O O C O A G
C Y I O U O C N C C O K A
D A O S S A L T A I E U N
T I X N Y H P A R G O I B
```

ANTHOLOGY
ATLAS
BIOGRAPHY
CATALOGUE
COMIC
COOKBOOK
DIARY
DICTIONARY
ENCYCLOPEDIA

GUIDEBOOK
NOVEL
POETRY BOOK
TEXTBOOK
THESAURUS

PUZZLE 111: TYPES OF STORY

```
M D L O O I E L A T Y R I A F
I C T S N A D V E N T U R E A
E M B C F A N C A M C Y E R R
I S I I L R C Y I Y A H S T B
Y H O E Y A Y C F P O H E Y A
R A G N E V C A V R E C N I O
E H R C A B B I R G N T E I E
T A A E O L F O R A R E R V R
S C P F E N R A M O B C I H E
Y T H I N E H O N A T T C A L
M I Y C I I R R I T C S S E T
C O B T L E B I M E A H I Y O
Y N C I O A T Y T O A S I H R
T I T O F M T E L Y C N Y A L
I P O N E H D E Y R T E O W I
```

ACTION
ADVENTURE
BIOGRAPHY
DETECTIVE
EPIC
FABLE
FAIRY TALE
FANTASY
HISTORICAL

HORROR
MYSTERY
MYTH
ROMANCE
SCIENCE FICTION

PUZZLE 112: WRITING

```
C L R O H P A T E M P A E
H C E E P S R E L A P L L
N S T P L S L E R E I G E
T O A A E C T A S M E L G
I G I P I T G E I S T N Y
E L I T E R N S T I I R P
R H R R A T Y N T L O A R
A A T P E U E A L T S E E
M T H N H T T E S S S G T
M E C A N E P C A S E S P
A E E O O S A G N T E T A
R E C E P P E H R U T A H
G N I C A P S R A H P U C
```

ARTICLE	PASSAGE
CHAPTER	PUNCTUATION
CONTENTS	SENTENCE
ESSAY	SIMILE
GRAMMAR	SPACING
LETTER	SPEECH
METAPHOR	SPELLING
PAGE	STORY
PARAGRAPH	TITLE

PUZZLE 113: GRAMMATICAL TERMS

```
E C M A U R P L U R A L U
N O I P N L C O N N U N N
U N R B U E R M E O U O S
O J N R O R R O R O I N R
N U P N N I C O N T U E R
R N N D O O R T I O N E A
E C A P R I C S N I I N L
P T J N P A O N M V M B U
O I C O R P O R P P R R G
R O N T E M E T N E R E N
P N S R M T I N V B R T I
S B P O E J E N P U T O S
A N C D E V I T C E J D A
```

ABSTRACT NOUN   SINGULAR
ADJECTIVE   VERB
COMMON NOUN
CONJUNCTION
DETERMINER
PLURAL
PREPOSITION
PRONOUN
PROPER NOUN

PUZZLE 114: PUNCTUATION

```
E M R P E S P O Y N M N N N L
P H P U X A O A E T O M S L Q
M Y H C C T Q M A L M S H R H
P P H M L H U S O M O A R A N
A H N A A S E C I P C A S S C
P E S Q M A S B C S T O E L C
O N P L A D T L R I P L M B A
S P E O T P I I E A D I O M O
T A E P I S O S H T C U L M A
R A C E O N N T B R A K O L K
O E H A N E M H S T R M E M E
P M M P M E A Q Y L T I S T I
H S A P A M R I R O L S X L R
E L R S R S K E C I S U H O P
O X K O K M O R E P C A F S H
```

APOSTROPHE
BRACKET
COLON
COMMA
DASH
ELLIPSIS
EXCLAMATION MARK
FULL STOP

HYPHEN
QUESTION MARK
SPEECH MARK

PUZZLE 115: PREPOSITIONS

Prepositions are words that tell you where or when something is in relation to something else.

```
A R O U N D E O R I H F F
A B O V E D T E N N G R O
O S O T I O V F E A U O P
N E S S W O R E T B O M O
I A T A T O W S B E R E T
P U R T N T E S E N H T N
O D X T E E T O H E T S O
S E O B D S I R I A O N T
N F A I D O S C N T W I S
S T S O F L O A D H O A O
O E W X O C P T T T O G X
B N I V M T P T T T X A E
D N O Y E B O H U N D E R
```

ABOVE	BEYOND	OUTSIDE
ACROSS	CLOSE TO	OVER
AGAINST	DOWN	PAST
AROUND	FROM	THROUGH
BEHIND	IN FRONT OF	TOWARDS
BENEATH	NEXT TO	UNDER
BESIDE	ON TOP OF	
BETWEEN	OPPOSITE	

PUZZLE 116: ABSTRACT NOUNS

An abstract noun refers to an idea or feeling, rather than a physical object that you can see and touch.

A	U	L	H	E	A	L	T	H	U	E	Y	G
N	H	T	G	N	E	R	T	S	A	R	E	Y
N	M	E	M	O	R	Y	C	E	E	K	T	C
F	O	D	P	F	S	I	S	V	C	S	R	E
R	K	I	A	I	T	S	A	D	E	C	Y	I
E	N	S	T	T	H	R	E	N	E	T	T	H
E	O	S	I	A	B	S	O	N	I	E	Y	N
D	W	S	E	R	N	H	D	S	D	E	P	T
O	L	E	N	F	E	I	O	N	E	N	L	S
M	E	C	C	U	K	I	G	C	E	R	I	S
O	D	C	E	N	R	E	A	A	T	I	W	K
N	G	U	T	U	I	E	I	E	M	I	R	A
N	E	S	C	S	P	C	L	N	M	I	E	F

BRAVERY   IMAGINATION   STRENGTH
CURIOSITY   KINDNESS   SUCCESS
FREEDOM   KNOWLEDGE
FRIENDSHIP   MEMORY
FUN   PATIENCE
HEALTH   PEACE
HONESTY   SPEED

PUZZLE 117: PROPER NOUNS

Proper nouns are people, places or things.

```
T I E E L L T T K D N
I T T E O E L R R T I V A
P T V N A N E I H S N I E
T E D R N T V O S E G E C
U O T V I E T E I R H E O
N H I P R L A R N E E A C
N D U N X S N O A V N N I
T J I J T J R C P E R A T
H L U E N O N I S T Y N N
E L R C J Y D X E N V E A
Y I R A I R K E T U I U L
Y A E P N T E M I O I R T
F R I D A Y N I N M I E A
```

ATLANTIC OCEAN	LONDON
EARTH	MEXICO
EASTER	MOUNT EVEREST
FRIDAY	RIVER NILE
JULY	SPANISH
JUPITER	
KING HENRY VIII	

PUZZLE 118: TIME-RELATED WORDS

```
E D H E R N L E E D U R I N G
E E N S Y A E L P A S T R F S
A U O U S A I H X F T S R I F
R N W T I H Y A T A B D M T R
L W L Y W L E E T E S U Y Y O
I Y L N L C E R V Y L O D P Y
E U A A N R E E L T N A R A U
R E N O E R N N A F E E D Y W
M I S T U T E N T R V R E O F
F C A T U D E Y L I E A R L Y
D L U A D O A A O T N R S A O
S F L U U D A U S O O A A L Y
U L S S O D S E O M A F T E R
Y L L T E L Y S O P I N E X T
L Y I S Y T E T E E R O F E B
```

AFTER   FUTURE   PREVIOUSLY
ALREADY   LASTLY   SIMULTANEOUSLY
BEFORE   LATER   SOON
DURING   MEANWHILE   SUDDENLY
EARLIER   NEXT   THEN
EVENTUALLY   NOW   TODAY
FINALLY   ONCE   TOMORROW
FIRST   PAST   YESTERDAY

PUZZLE 119: NOISES

```
B U Z Z S I O C G N A B M
C H C L E U Q S R N C E O
R R A A S B R H C A A R O
E R T W L E L R S R S L B
N U I Z T N A E A A L H C
I S N T B C H C E A L S B
H T A N K L S C Z P W P L
W L R L R M A B N H A R S
C E E P A R C S I U A C I
R R U M B L E S T T R C Z
I T H U M P T N T E Z C Z
H K T M R L N L S L A M L
W B B C E Z E Z Z I F T E
```

BANG	CRASH	SLAM
BLAST	CRUNCH	SPLASH
BLEEP	FIZZ	SQUELCH
BOOM	RATTLE	SWISH
BUZZ	RUMBLE	THUMP
CLANG	RUSTLE	WHINE
CLATTER	SCRAPE	WHIR
CRACKLE	SIZZLE	WHISTLE

PUZZLE 120: PRONOUNS

Pronouns replace the name of a person or thing in a sentence.

```
Y   W   Y   E   S   H   E
E   O   N   Y   Y   I   I
U   I   E   H   H   R   H
M   H   I   H   M   U   H
T   M   E   H   E   O   M
U   R   I   E   H   T   Y
S   T   H   U   T   E   H
```

HER	THEIR
HIM	THEM
HIS	THEY
IT	US
MINE	WE
MY	YOU
OUR	
SHE	

PUZZLE 121: TRAVEL WORDS

```
V S Y L I T R A P E D A N
E T I T L R J O U R N E Y
E A S R K G A C A O E G O
S X L E A V E F I U T S O
E V P K E H G T A R S A N
V O R E I C A E O S E E E
I Y T K D N N P I S T S T
R A E E I I S A I N T R A
R G H T E N T U T P H E G
A E S V A L R I I S G V I
F E V R V C C R O E I O V
D Y T V A E T Y R N L D A
D D R I V E A K C E F Y N
```

ARRIVE
CRUISE
CYCLE
DEPART
DESTINATION
DISTANCE
DRIVE
EXPEDITION

FLIGHT
HIKE
JOURNEY
LEAVE
NAVIGATE
OVERSEAS
SAFARI
SAIL

TRANSPORT
TREK
TRIP
VOYAGE

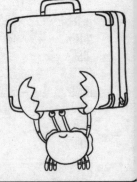

PUZZLE 122: BODY PARTS

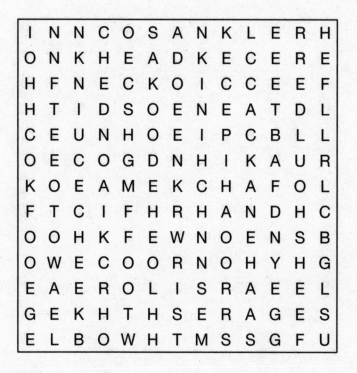

```
I N N C O S A N K L E R H
O N K H E A D K E C E R E
H F N E C K O I C C E E F
H T I D S O E N E A T D L
C E U N H O E I P C B L L
O E C O G D N H I K A U R
K O E A M E K C H A F O L
F T C I F H R H A N D H C
O O H K F E W N O E N S B
O W E C O O R N O H Y H G
E A E R O L I S R A E E L
G E K H T H S E R A G E S
E L B O W H T M S S G F U
```

ANKLE	FACE	MOUTH
ARM	FINGER	NECK
BACK	FOOT	NOSE
CHEEK	HAND	SHOULDER
CHIN	HEAD	TOE
EARS	HIP	WRIST
ELBOW	KNEE	
EYES	LEG	

PUZZLE 123: 2D SHAPES

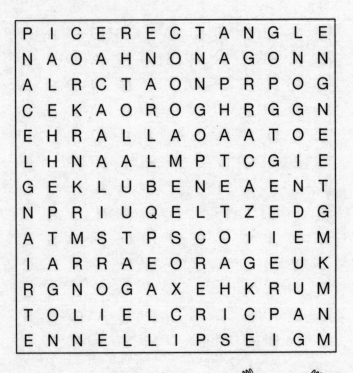

```
P I C E R E C T A N G L E
N A O A H N O N A G O N N
A L R C T A O N P R P O G
C E K A O R O G H R G G N
E H R A L L A O A A T O E
L H N A A L M P T C G I E
G E K L U B E N E A E N T
N P R I U Q E L T Z E D G
A T M S T P S C O I I E M
I A R R A E O R A G E U K
R G N O G A X E H K R U M
T O L I E L C R I C P A N
E N N E L L I P S E I G M
```

CIRCLE
DECAGON
ELLIPSE
HEPTAGON
HEXAGON
KITE
NONAGON
OCTAGON

PARALLELOGRAM
PENTAGON
RECTANGLE
RHOMBUS
SQUARE
TRAPEZIUM
TRIANGLE

PUZZLE 124: 3D SHAPES

```
T O H A D C C P H O D C D
O E R E H P S H C A O R L
C M T E P O P T A N D I N
S D D R O N A D E O C I C
E U I M A H E O I O R Y U
D S N M E H O O S O L M D
M N R D A Y E A Y I B I R
O O R O R R H D N P U U C
C O C N S E Y D R M A U C
N E O R D Y E P R O B C I
A D N R N R C E O E N C A
O N O R D E H A C E D O D
A N D E N O O O R E C H I
```

CONE
CUBE
CUBOID
CYLINDER
DODECAHEDRON
ICOSAHEDRON
OCTAHEDRON
PRISM

PYRAMID
SPHERE
TETRAHEDRON

PUZZLE 125: HOMOPHONES 1

Homophones are words that sound the same as each other, but have different meanings. In puzzles 125 to 130, choose the correct word from the CAPITALIZED options, and then find that word in the wordsearch grid. The first one has been done for you as an example.

The solutions are listed at the back of the book.

a) The princess had many different clothes to WARE / WEAR / WHERE.

b) I have never BEAN / BEEN to London.

c) The dog was wagging its TAIL / TALE.

d) The students brought in pencil cases containing their new STATIONARY / STATIONERY.

e) There were two pieces of fruit in the bowl: an apple and a PAIR / PARE / PEAR.

f) I thought I had five slices of pizza, but there were only FOR / FORE / FOUR.

g) After lunch today I had dessert, which was a chocolate MOOSE / MOUSSE.

h) I think the car park is just over THEIR / THERE / THEY'RE.

E	R	S	L	Z	V	Y	Q	F	C
U	S	A	C	K	C	R	N	P	H
G	E	S	E	A	N	E	R	I	W
Q	K	R	U	P	Z	N	W	N	N
W	V	J	E	O	M	O	V	C	A
R	U	O	F	H	M	I	N	A	D
I	A	W	G	F	T	T	A	X	B
Z	I	F	E	J	A	A	T	N	E
T	A	I	L	A	Y	T	X	X	E
Y	U	T	H	L	R	S	C	H	N

PUZZLE 126: HOMOPHONES 2

For instructions, see puzzle 125.

a) The students at the back of the classroom couldn't see the **BOARD / BORED**.

b) I only had dinner an hour ago but I can't remember what we **ATE / EIGHT**.

c) I want to play guitar in a **BAND / BANNED**.

d) The bakers ran out of **FLOUR / FLOWER**.

e) When making bread, you have to **NEED / KNEAD / KNEED** the dough.

f) In mathematics classes, we have tests on subtraction and **ADDITION / EDITION**.

g) Male sheep are called rams, and female sheep are called **EWES / USE / YEWS**.

h) The boy wanted to send his friend a letter, but he didn't know how to **RIGHT / WRITE**.

B	A	G	K	N	E	A	D	E	Q
H	U	F	D	M	D	N	A	B	T
B	N	U	E	A	T	E	P	X	C
T	B	O	H	T	X	U	P	C	E
J	E	O	I	J	I	A	V	W	U
J	D	L	A	T	H	R	E	H	C
Q	U	K	M	R	I	S	W	R	L
R	H	Z	U	P	D	D	V	Y	G
F	P	N	H	V	X	P	D	Y	Q
C	V	F	L	O	U	R	Q	A	M

PUZZLE 127: HOMOPHONES 3

For instructions, see puzzle 125.

a) The ferocious lion shook his **MAIN / MANE**.

b) Beside the pond sat a large, warty **TOAD / TOED / TOWED**.

c) Whenever there is a draw, neither team will have **ONE / WON**.

d) The musician sat at the piano and played a **CHORD / CORD / CORED**.

e) He forgot to write an address on the letter that he **CENT / SCENT / SENT**.

f) The lemonade jug was full, so it was difficult to **POOR / PORE / POUR**.

g) Last night I saw a spider in my room, high up on the **CEILING / SEALING**.

h) I was invited to a party, but I don't know if **AISLE / I'LL / ISLE** go.

P	N	C	N	L	I	P	D	S	L
M	M	E	L	E	O	D	E	I	T
G	E	I	I	U	A	I	O	G	O
T	R	L	R	O	N	I	I	I	C
E	I	I	T	T	E	L	T	N	H
H	A	N	L	L	N	G	W	P	O
O	N	G	T	C	A	N	E	O	R
W	I	N	C	L	M	D	I	H	D
S	E	E	E	N	N	N	O	W	D
S	C	T	N	T	E	P	O	E	R

PUZZLE 128: HOMOPHONES 4

For instructions, see puzzle 125.

a) Some people are nice, and some people AREN'T / AUNT.

b) Everyone went on the trip ACCEPT / EXCEPT me.

c) If students try to cheat on tests they will get CAUGHT / COURT.

d) I told my friend a joke to cheer her up, but it had the opposite AFFECT / EFFECT.

e) Being a vegetarian means that you don't eat MEAT / MEET / METE.

f) The shop assistant wrapped the vase carefully so that it would not BRAKE / BREAK.

g) The person who prayed each day was very HOLEY / HOLY / WHOLLY.

h) The footballer aimed for the goal but he MISSED / MIST.

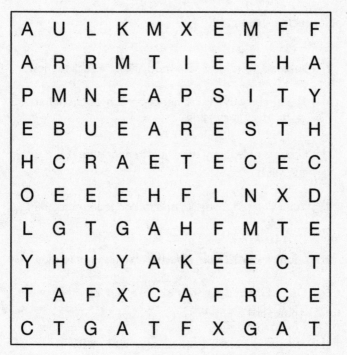

A	U	L	K	M	X	E	M	F	F
A	R	R	M	T	I	E	E	H	A
P	M	N	E	A	P	S	I	T	Y
E	B	U	E	A	R	E	S	T	H
H	C	R	A	E	T	E	C	E	C
O	E	E	E	H	F	L	N	X	D
L	G	T	G	A	H	F	M	T	E
Y	H	U	Y	A	K	E	E	C	T
T	A	F	X	C	A	F	R	C	E
C	T	G	A	T	F	X	G	A	T

PUZZLE 129: HOMOPHONES 5

For instructions, see puzzle 125.

a) It rained yesterday, so nobody MODE / MOWED the lawn.

b) The queen was kind to her citizens throughout her entire RAIN / REIGN / REIN.

c) I have a hole in my shoe, just beneath the HEAL / HEEL / HE'LL.

d) You will need a needle and thread to learn to SEW / SO / SOW.

e) I don't know WEATHER / WHETHER I will go out to play.

f) One of these diamonds is a fake, but the other one is REAL / REEL.

g) The people in the queue had to WAIT / WEIGHT.

h) My baby brother was very upset and started to BALL / BAWL.

```
J D L V Q S N U N Q
J S L W A B Z B D H
L W T I A D N W R C
L E H G O H E E F Z
W A E E Q D I W M U
E X E H T G F X O K
S Y Y R N H T G I M
P V T F C S E I F V
C T I A N V C R A F
G W X O K T X Q A W
```

PUZZLE 130: HOMOPHONES 6

For instructions, see puzzle 125.

a) In the woods I saw a brown BARE / BEAR.

b) The postman said hello as he walked PASSED / PAST.

c) The cowboy ROAD / RODE / ROWED a horse.

d) The man was turned into an ogre by the evil WHICH / WITCH.

e) The people in the boat rowed using an AWE / OAR / OR / ORE.

f) I turned up the volume so I could HEAR / HERE.

g) The person who admired themselves in the mirror every day was very VAIN / VANE / VEIN.

h) The football match was GRATE / GREAT.

B	A	G	G	W	G	R	E	A	T
H	A	S	H	O	E	I	A	D	A
R	E	T	D	R	G	H	I	I	E
H	H	W	T	P	A	E	T	H	D
R	D	I	S	A	B	A	A	H	A
A	R	T	A	A	R	V	R	G	A
O	A	C	P	O	D	A	A	R	E
C	B	H	D	A	E	E	A	I	I
H	W	E	A	H	I	E	A	A	N
O	I	R	R	T	B	I	E	O	H

PUZZLE 131: MISSPELLINGS 1

In puzzles 131 to 133, choose the correct spelling from the CAPITALIZED options, and then find the correctly spelled word in the wordsearch grid. The first one has been done for you as an example.

The solutions are listed at the back of the book.

a) I don't like when the team I support LOOSE / <u>LOSE</u>.

b) Three men rode on camels across the sandy DESERT / DESSERT.

c) My family moved house so now we have a new ADDRESS / ADRESS.

d) Birthday presents are often a SUPRISE / SURPRISE.

e) The month after January is FEBRUARY / FEBUARY.

f) When writing, it's important to use good GRAMMAR / GRAMMER.

g) The students were bored by the lesson and were not showing any INTEREST / INTREST.

h) Some spelling tests are easy and some are DIFFICULT / DIFICULT.

```
Y  S  S  A  E  D  D  S  S  L  L  A
L  E  U  Y  R  A  U  R  B  E  F  N
R  S  L  R  M  O  M  D  I  S  F  S
I  D  F  D  P  N  F  E  I  R  D  S
I  Y  R  F  I  R  E  L  S  S  R  E
Y  N  D  E  G  F  I  P  I  O  S  R
D  T  T  E  I  R  F  S  O  R  L  D
S  R  L  E  S  S  A  I  E  R  N  D
R  I  S  I  R  E  E  M  C  S  S  A
T  S  T  A  D  E  R  D  M  U  F  R
R  S  S  S  L  C  S  T  E  A  L  I
R  B  F  R  F  E  A  T  R  L  R  T
```

PUZZLE 132: MISSPELLINGS 2

For instructions, see puzzle 131.

- **a)** Polar bears are large, white animals which live in the ARCTIC / ARTIC.

- **b)** Do you prefer your POTATOES / POTATOS mashed or baked?

- **c)** You shouldn't run in corridors unless it's absolutely NECCESSARY / NECESSARY.

- **d)** The university professor was very INTELLIGENT / INTELIGENT.

- **e)** A fact is something which is DEFINITELY / DEFINITLEY true.

- **f)** After the boy lost his watch, his parents were DISAPPOINTED / DISSAPPOINTED.

- **g)** Nobody laughed at their joke, so they were EMBARASSED / EMBARRASSED.

- **h)** The party guests are running late, but they are ALLMOST / ALMOST ready.

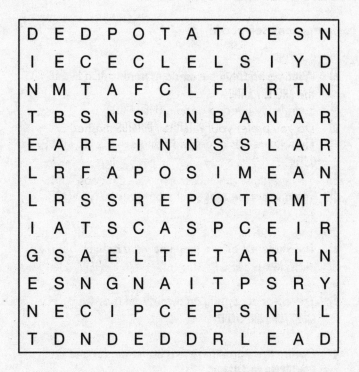

```
D E D P O T A T O E S N
I E C E C L E L S I Y D
N M T A F C L F I R T N
T B S N S I N B A N A R
E A R E I N N S S L A R
L R F A P O S I M E A N
L R S S R E P O T R M T
I A T S C A S P C E I R
G S A E L T E T A R L N
E S N G N A I T P S R Y
N E C I P C E P S N I L
T D N D E D D R L E A D
```

PUZZLE 133: MISSPELLINGS 3

For instructions, see puzzle 131.

a) Winning an Olympic medal is hard to ACHEIVE / ACHIEVE.

b) Everybody needs a good FREIND / FRIEND.

c) There were lots of people waiting in the CUE / QEUE / QUEUE.

d) Tea and coffee look similar but taste very DIFFARENT / DIFFERENT / DIFFRENT.

e) The student claimed they knew the answer, but they didn't REALLY / REALY.

f) The actor accepting an award said they were very GRATEFUL / GREATFUL.

g) During the storm there was both thunder and LIGHTENING / LIGHTNING.

h) It's helpful to write down important dates in a CALANDER / CALENDAR.

```
E F A T L L N R Y E N D
G R L C Q E Y I C L G A
R F E E H L I A G N H T
A N L R E I A L I D N F
T Q T L E R E N N E R R
E N L E F I T V R I F A
F U F D Q H G E E R Y D
U N E U G H F N E E E N
L Q E I R F D L R A R E
H U L F I I R U F L Q L
E G E D A U I H D L F A
N E T E Y A L A U Y E C
```

PUZZLE 134: ANAGRAM PAIRS 1

An anagram is another word that uses the same set of letters, but in a different order. In puzzles 134 to 138, find a suitable anagram of the CAPITALIZED word, and then find that word in the wordsearch grid. Each anagram must be one that can be placed in the gap in its sentence.

For example, in the sentence 'The RIDER stayed _ _ _ _ _ when she wore a coat', you could rearrange the letters RIDER to spell DRIER, making the sentence 'The RIDER stayed DRIER when she wore a coat.'

a) I am going to have a NAP when I finish washing this dirty frying P̲A̲N̲.

b) I drank some hot chocolate from a MUG and then bought some chewing _ _ _.

c) Can you pass me that paint POT which has no lid on _ _ _ ?

d) I SAW a film last night, which _ _ _ about a girl in space.

e) If you turn on the television NOW you will find out who _ _ _ the football match.

f) They caught TEN fish by using their _ _ _.

g) I can see a large OWL nesting on a _ _ _ branch of that tree.

h) WHO did you buy the gift for, and _ _ _ much did it cost?

O M P L U O N

H O O T O A O

T P M E P A S

M U W N L W A

G N O A W O W

O U H O N A W

O O M N S L S T

PUZZLE 135: ANAGRAM PAIRS 2

For instructions, see puzzle 134.

a) He used the _ _ _ _ to wash the ink off his **SKIN**.

b) My kitten was stung by a **WASP** on both of her front
   _ _ _ _.

c) I touched a thorn on a **ROSE** and now my finger is
   _ _ _ _.

d) The tailor used scissors to **SNIP** the fabric, then fixed it
   together with safety _ _ _ _.

e) I tried to collect water from the **LAKE** but my bucket
   started to _ _ _ _.

f) I rolled a **DICE** to decide how my birthday cake should
   be _ _ _ _.

g) The wizard woke up at the crack of **DAWN** and cast a
   spell with his magic _ _ _ _.

h) My little brother called me a rude **NAME** which I thought
   was very _ _ _ _.

W	E	A	A	A	W	S
A	S	K	A	E	L	D
N	E	O	S	O	E	S
D	A	N	R	C	P	I
S	I	E	I	E	A	N
P	C	W	M	A	W	K
E	E	A	A	A	S	E

PUZZLE 136: ANAGRAM PAIRS 3

For instructions, see puzzle 134.

a) The conductor made a SIGN for the choir to begin
to ____.

b) Every day when I WAKE up I like to drink a cup of
____ juice.

c) When I step in mud I have to wash my SHOE with the
garden ____.

d) I saw a FLEA sitting on a fallen ____.

e) PART of my shoe got caught in a mouse ____.

f) I was once told an unusual TALE about a ghost who
haunted people ____ at night.

g) I don't CARE that I lost the sprint ____ because I had
fun taking part.

h) We are going to use the water in this BOWL to ____
bubbles.

```
T R A P W I A
R A L E S F N
R R A I W R E
L K N O A S L
A G L C O E O
T B E H A L T
E F P F E C R
```

PUZZLE 137: ANAGRAM PAIRS 4

For instructions, see puzzle 134.

a) At the playground I sat on the **SWING** and pretended I was a plane with _ _ _ _ _.

b) A man and his **HORSE** galloped along the sandy _ _ _ _ _.

c) My grandma always **KNITS** me special socks because she says my feet _ _ _ _ _.

d) The ancient Romans wore **TOGAS** and sometimes kept _ _ _ _ _ on their farms.

e) The workman used his box of **TOOLS** to fix the broken leg on the wooden _ _ _ _ _.

f) In our fruit bowl we have both a yellow **LEMON** and a large _ _ _ _ _.

g) Once upon a time **THERE** were _ _ _ _ _ little pigs.

h) My dad **LOVES** to watch TV shows in which detectives _ _ _ _ _ mysteries.

S	G	N	I	W	M	K
E	O	O	L	E	N	S
S	R	S	L	I	S	T
O	A	O	T	T	O	O
L	N	S	H	A	W	O
V	I	I	W	S	O	L
E	E	R	H	T	O	G

PUZZLE 138: ANAGRAM PAIRS 5

For instructions, see puzzle 134.

a) I was under the **IMPRESSION** that my parents had given me _ _ _ _ _ _ _ _ _ _ to go to the party.

b) The cake was an amazing **CREATION** but it caused an allergic _ _ _ _ _ _ _ _.

c) The **PRINCE** caught the crab which had nipped him with its _ _ _ _ _ _.

d) I wanted to watch a TV show about a **METEOR**, but I couldn't find the _ _ _ _ _ _.

e) It was clear from the **REPLAYS** that the football team only had ten _ _ _ _ _ _ _.

f) I love to go to fancy-dress **PARTIES** where we all dress up as swashbuckling _ _ _ _ _ _ _.

g) The homework was **FIENDISH** so I was glad when it was _ _ _ _ _ _ _ _.

h) The pack of young **SPANIELS** nipped at my hand, but it didn't hurt – it was _ _ _ _ _ _ _ _.

```
I  R  Y  I  O  P  S  R  P  S
R  O  L  F  S  E  E  F  E  I
E  E  T  E  T  A  I  T  R  S
C  Y  A  A  C  N  O  P  M  S
N  P  R  T  I  M  R  L  I  E
I  I  I  S  E  R  E  A  S  L
P  O  H  R  P  I  E  Y  S  N
N  E  I  R  A  R  N  E  I  I
D  P  L  P  P  P  S  R  O  A
E  P  P  E  H  P  A  S  N  P
```

PUZZLE 139: ANTONYMS 1

An antonym of a word is a word which has the opposite meaning.

In puzzles 139 to 144, work out the antonym of each CAPITALIZED word, and then find that word in the wordsearch grid. The first one is solved for you, as an example.

The solutions are listed at the back of the book.

a) The giant had big arms and was very ~~WEAK~~ <u>STRONG</u>.

b) It was decided that the lion would remain CAPTIVE _ _ _ _.

c) The hikers wanted to walk to the lake but it was too NEAR _ _ _.

d) Nocturnal animals are active during the DAY _ _ _ _ _.

e) The sun was shining INSIDE _ _ _ _ _ _ _.

f) The bridge was falling apart and did not feel DANGEROUS _ _ _ _ _.

g) Birthdays are important dates to FORGET _ _ _ _ _ _ _ _.

h) The scientists had different ideas and could not DISAGREE _ _ _ _ _ _.

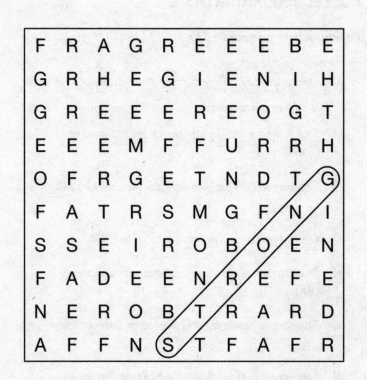

```
F  R  A  G  R  E  E  E  B  E
G  R  H  E  G  I  E  N  I  H
G  R  E  E  E  R  E  O  G  T
E  E  E  M  F  F  U  R  R  H
O  F  R  G  E  T  N  D  T  G
F  A  T  R  S  M  G  F  N  I
S  S  E  I  R  O  B  O  E  N
F  A  D  E  E  N  R  E  F  E
N  E  R  O  B  T  R  A  R  D
A  F  F  N  S  T  F  A  F  R
```

PUZZLE 140: ANTONYMS 2

For instructions, see puzzle 139.

a) Under the bridge lived a troll that was famed for its BEAUTY _ _ _ _ _ _ _ _.

b) The princess who fought the dragon was very COWARDLY _ _ _ _ _.

c) The boy fell off his bike and got his clothes CLEAN _ _ _ _ _.

d) Every number in the two times table is ODD _ _ _ _.

e) The curtains were closed, so the room was very LIGHT _ _ _ _.

f) The rooster woke up and started to crow at DUSK _ _ _ _.

g) I searched for hours, but the bracelet was never LOST _ _ _ _ _.

h) The criminal who robbed the bank was INNOCENT _ _ _ _ _ _.

U	U	L	B	L	N	K	D	U	K
V	E	F	E	A	Y	R	I	E	N
N	E	S	N	V	R	A	R	E	I
Y	V	W	S	W	E	D	T	T	F
N	A	I	I	E	I	N	Y	U	O
D	R	Y	U	B	N	T	N	O	U
D	B	E	N	E	L	I	R	N	N
Y	I	Y	A	I	U	U	L	R	D
G	A	L	U	K	O	I	I	G	N
E	S	G	E	E	G	A	N	N	U

PUZZLE 141: ANTONYMS 3

For instructions, see puzzle 139.

a) I had to clean my room because it was very
TIDY _ _ _ _ _.

b) Whenever it rained, the laundry hanging outside
became DRY _ _ _.

c) The fence was too high for anyone to climb
UNDER _ _ _ _ it.

d) The family who lived in the castle were very
POOR _ _ _ _.

e) The famous basketball player was very SHORT _ _ _ _ _.

f) The audience were excited for the concert to
FINISH _ _ _ _ _.

g) The mountain path was dangerous, so the group had to
stay APART _ _ _ _ _ _ _ _.

h) My rabbit ate a lot of lettuce and became very
THIN _ _ _.

```
T G A W H A E F G O
R E H T E G O T R T
O E O S A S A E T R
S R F A T Y V O R S
S A C H O O T C R H
R T R A T S L I S O
G A W Y H L C W O S
A E T E A H T T T T
T E T T M L A H F S
A R C E Y S S E M T
```

PUZZLE 142: ANTONYMS 4

For instructions, see puzzle 139.

a) After the engine was repaired the train started moving BACKWARD _ _ _ _ _ _ _.

b) The pupils were called to a meeting if their exam results were too GOOD _ _ _.

c) The bunch of flowers made the old man SAD _ _ _ _ _.

d) The group climbed a mountain and took lots of pictures at the BOTTOM _ _ _.

e) The astronauts' mission had been a FAILURE _ _ _ _ _ _ _.

f) The tough arithmetic quiz had been very EASY

_ _ _ _ _ _ _ _ _.

g) Once the doors to the elevator had closed it started to go DOWN _ _.

h) The boy with red shoes finished in LAST _ _ _ _ _ place.

```
F  S  F  O  R  W  A  R  D  R
L  D  T  I  O  F  C  B  E  R
L  I  A  R  C  R  A  S  S  F
Y  F  F  S  U  C  C  E  S  S
P  F  O  F  D  C  I  I  Y  P
P  I  O  U  I  U  S  T  F  A
A  C  U  U  O  R  D  F  O  P
H  U  U  Y  S  B  S  C  Y  P
D  L  Y  P  A  F  U  T  T  S
C  T  T  D  R  O  U  W  R  I
```

PUZZLE 143: ANTONYMS 5

For instructions, see puzzle 139.

a) I like to have a shower every day AFTER _ _ _ _ _ _ school.

b) The bowl of tomato soup was served COLD _ _ _.

c) When I arrived at the house, the door was CLOSED _ _ _ _.

d) The bottle of milk in the fridge was EMPTY _ _ _ _.

e) The sunflowers in the field had started to SHRINK _ _ _ _.

f) The holiday swimming pool was very SHALLOW _ _ _ _.

g) The pillow on the prince's bed was too SOFT _ _ _ _.

h) The new lampshade meant that the room was very DIM _ _ _ _ _ _.

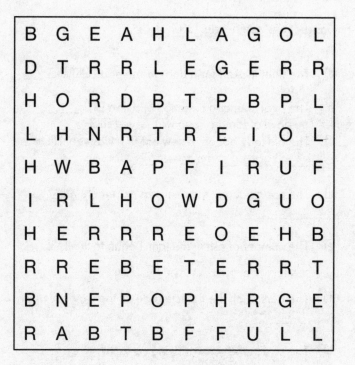

```
B  G  E  A  H  L  A  G  O  L
D  T  R  R  L  E  G  E  R  R
H  O  R  D  B  T  P  B  P  L
L  H  N  R  T  R  E  I  O  L
H  W  B  A  P  F  I  R  U  F
I  R  L  H  O  W  D  G  U  O
H  E  R  R  R  E  O  E  H  B
R  R  E  B  E  T  E  R  R  T
B  N  E  P  O  P  H  R  G  E
R  A  B  T  B  F  F  U  L  L
```

PUZZLE 144: ANTONYMS 6

For instructions, see puzzle 139.

a)   The thief looked for a door to use as an ENTRANCE _ _ _ _.

b)   The pilot changed direction and flew EAST _ _ _ _.

c)   The old lady bought a new hat that was very CHEAP
     _ _ _ _ _ _ _ _.

d)   The bridge across the river was extremely WIDE
     _ _ _ _ _ _.

e)   The number of fish in the tank began to DECREASE
     _ _ _ _ _ _ _ _.

f)   The person on the tricycle rode all the way over HERE
     _ _ _ _ _.

g)   The bird in the sky was flying very LOW _ _ _ _.

h)   I thought that our homework this week was very
     INTERESTING _ _ _ _ _ _ _.

E	E	E	N	G	E	I	I	A	R
E	X	X	S	I	T	S	E	W	T
E	S	I	P	X	E	I	S	G	H
E	X	A	T	E	X	I	N	R	E
H	B	N	E	T	N	I	O	T	R
R	X	A	H	R	R	S	R	E	R
R	R	R	E	O	C	C	I	G	O
I	E	R	B	I	I	N	R	V	H
E	R	O	I	E	H	G	I	H	E
I	T	W	O	I	E	I	B	N	O

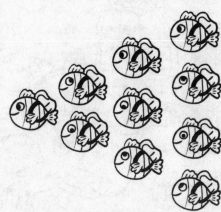

All of the
ANSWERS

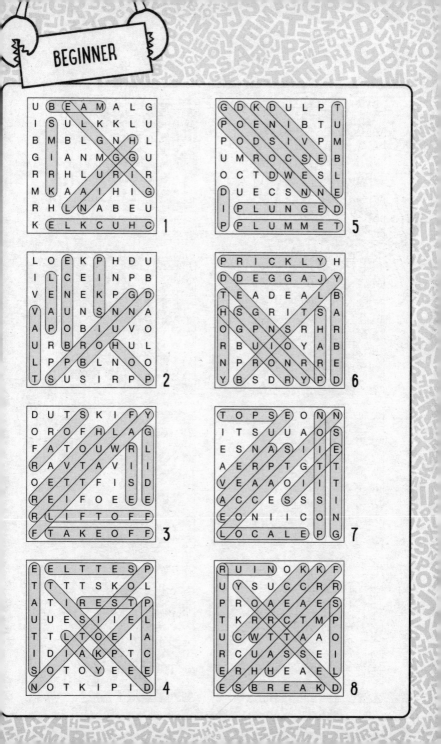

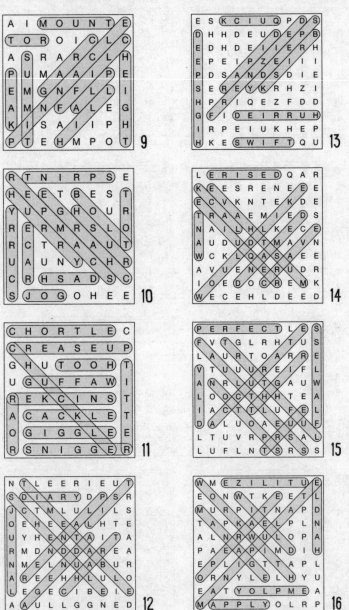

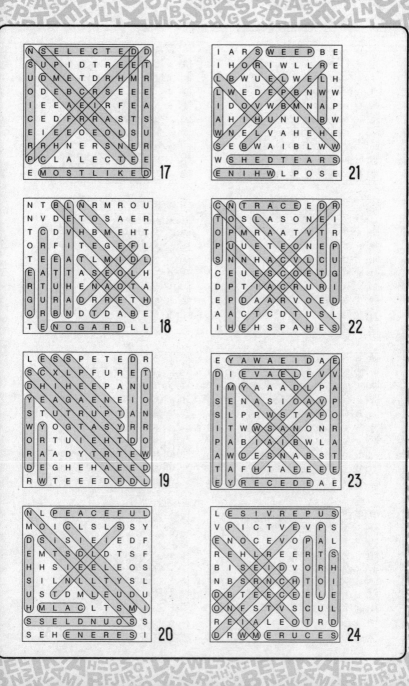

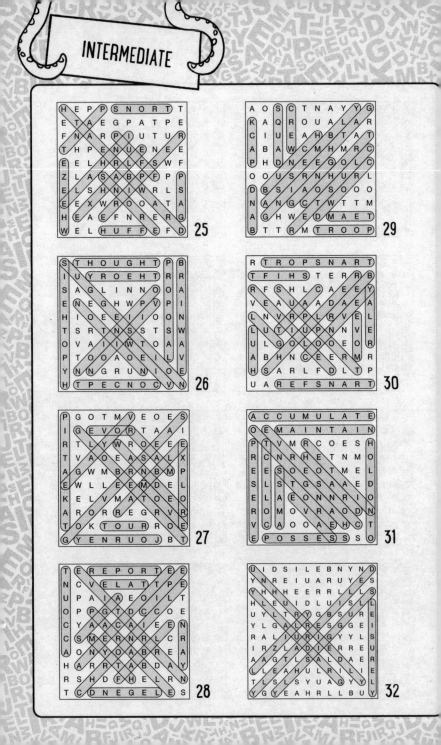

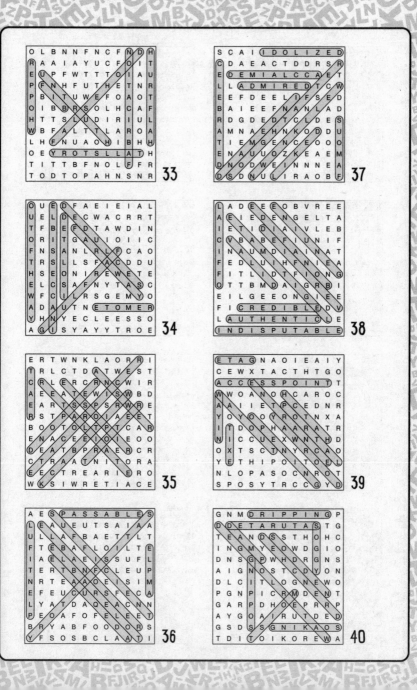

Word search puzzles 41–48

41
```
E U D R G Y E E L H B C
L D O O L O D N F L U G
I U E R L T R R S R N E
T R F S E G S D U I U R
I A S R D S U U T T U R
U B O R E I I S B A S Y
L L L R W W A L D O A D
G E I B R L O L I S R R
R U D G G A E P I E U A
H L S N U H G U O T N H
E I O R S E O R L U R T
L L W R S E R U C E S U
```

45
```
I I C C O M P A C T E E
M T E E Y E Y L T E P L
E I E R M E P P E M E U
V S C E U I N O C I L C
I N E R N T T I R N T S
M E E L O Y A E A U T U
T U T M Y S I I M T I N
E I O I T N C T N E L I
V P L E T M I O U I I M
M I P U M E M T P N M I
E U O P M E P E L I L C
D I M I N U T I V E C I
```

42
```
P L E A S A N T H O Y D
L D F L O V E L Y E E N
D D S T I E C G L R Y G
E N W L S G N G U L N A
L G E L P K L T D I G G
I M E O Y S A N M E C R
G T N A N E R N K L E
H R R P D I A I I R N E
T Y L O R H A N V N G A
F L O F C L D E A G F B
U G L A T D A E E U R L
L T A G L R R U L T C E
```

46
```
D U D U O T U T T O T I
E E N E E E D N N R D N
T D C A C H I E A C E D
C U E T T N N P S H I E
E N D T N T A E C T D P
N R L I A E A T R T I E
N E N O S C R C S T A N
O L I I D T H E H I T D
C A T E A L I E F E D E
S T E T N T E N D F D N
I E E A U I D D C S I T
D D T C I S O L A T E D
```

43
```
A G T I T T O E T N V R
F O G N I N N U T S E A
G O I E O N G T T T T D
Y D E S I R G R I T L E
T L X V I O I S R O S L
T O C R S K I A V U Y I
E R O O L I U C E O N D
R K X N Q T L E O Y O H
P I G X I Y G G T S T T
G N E V S R E L K S R F
H G E T O I T D L R O U
R G I G T N A I D A R L
```

47
```
S G A I C P U K C I P G
S U T H T G E S U E E C
S Y U R A R I A S T A O
K B M N X I A E E T U S M
M G E U D E T H C T G P
A A Q O E E X E O D R N R
T C B D T H R O A I T E
A Y S S A P G S X E U H
N H D N O S P K T Q O E
A R G U E R A N T A Y N
E O K G T T B U C O N D
F O R E T S A M R E B D
```

44
```
A C U S T O M A R I L Y
R S N A N U I R D M O L
Y T A R M K I O Y O Y Y
Y L T R D C U L U S M L
L U I Y U B L S S T U L
E I N R T L U S U O S A
O O K L A A E A E F B C
N A E E L N C T T T S I
R S D L L I I S E U P Y
S O Y E T Y Y D L N Y Y
N O R M A L L Y R L T T
K E G A R E V A N O S A
```

48
```
O C I R O T S I H E R P
S L N D G T A L R I A H
D C D D E R N D E S A D
G E D F C D S E T C E D
I T T H A G O I I T I A
N D A A E S T M A C I C
I I R M U S H D T C N N
C A L A P Q T I L U A A
G R S R D I I H O O O T
A R I I E T E T D N D E
E M I A G A G E N Q E O
E H E G A T N I V A C D
```

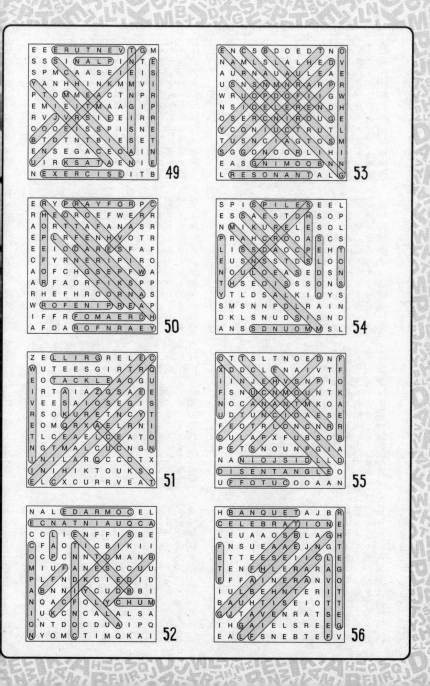

Word search puzzles.

Puzzle 57
```
D T C E V O K E W I E
R N B C O C E U T E E L
E W I R E N L K I I E D
T R T M I L J G C V R N
R I R T I O N L U E E I
I L E R C T G O R R T K
E S E M V I G B C E E E
V U O I E E L N A E U R
E M O I E M R E I C R P
U M E V E D B R E R K L
B O K V I O C E B M B O
R N U I C E V R R R I I
```

Puzzle 58
```
I K L L H S R O C M A M
A R L O R E L L O H A S
S A R K E T A L L E C E
W B A E R N C L R K O H
M E O I L A W C W L C M
R R R R L R S O L S S W
E E Y H R H A E L S O L
Y C E S R O L O A L W E
E R S C L L R L O E O
E O C L B H L L H E M B
B R A O E E E A L S M L
E C I O V Y M E S I A R
```

Puzzle 59
```
Z T K S T A R E A T R E
S A T R S M A B V V E A
C A T C H S I G H T O F
Z A S H E V R E S B O A
T L S A E N I D S A R Y
A G U R M N I G C T I A
K S R E S O A M A A R E
O S V P W Z N R A A F O
O E E M E E I G X C S
L C Y A R E I R T P E P
T R T K P I T V O O E G
O D D R A G E R R R R L
```

Puzzle 60
```
R U E M E T R T T G E H
E S I E E E C S R I I O
P S R N T E R O H E S M
S O G T A T A E R O U T
I Y C I T N X H D R U S
H R A O S C X L M C S T
W C O N L X E U O E E S
L M U A I Y R A R X L M
U T I T H E P S N H I
U M E U T N X I H I M U
U S L M E E G T S S N E
L R T E O H R S L X O I
```

Puzzle 61
```
A H E O M D R C E R F A
C R E A T E O M F A S G
D N K I P M O A S S O E
E E U A P C B H E N E C
V I H O C R I M O S C U
I S S R I O B N S B A D
S E E C N L A E I H E O
E C A I E H S F E I M R P
S T N G I S E D S A R P
E C O N S T R U C T O E
U E M O F R O R C L F A
C E R U T C A F U N A M
```

Puzzle 62
```
D I S T I N G U I S H I
E B C P E N W E I V O D
R P I I E Y S D R E T N
I S N P G S E I V E R T
E O S B E N P R N E E T
N E S S T R E M C T I U O
R O V I E S C O I N V O
E I F V B N G E O L V E
C V Y I O I N T T I S G K
S R C I I M I I P V R A
I S E Z I C T Y W O E M
D N E T E E C S P O T P
```

Puzzle 63
```
T O G A I N T R E P I D
L T N A L L A G R Y H G
T I D E T E R M I N E D
Y C O U R A G E O U S F
G K D N N G N U V G E D
U K C D H C G A C A F L
T L C U I E L N R N S O
S L N O L I A L E T B
Y L R S A P E R L R U H
A E A N S S N R T L A S
H S T E S R H F E E L D
D A U N T L E S S G D P
```

Puzzle 64
```
S S E S Y L R E D R O D
S P R H S G Y C E M E E
H R I S L P E C O R L I
I I H C E D H R E B M H
P S E A K S G T A M E S
S T R M E A T T A I S T
H I O R N U N C R E M H
A N F I L E U D L A I E
E P Z C S L I T S E M N
E N E A L O E F P A S
D U R T R P T A E N A N
U P E P S S P S L E K N
```

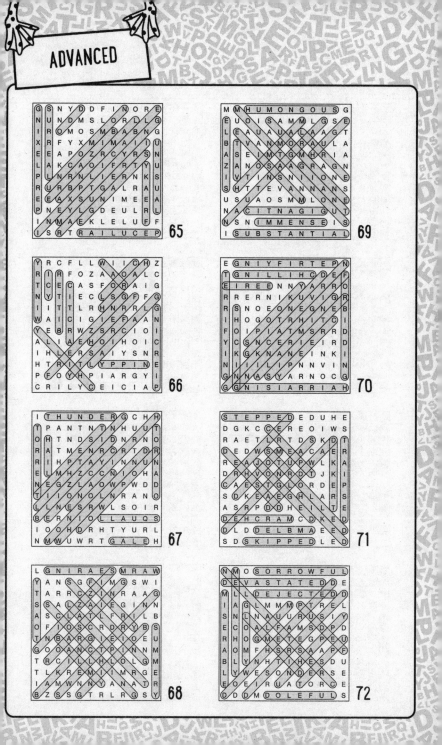

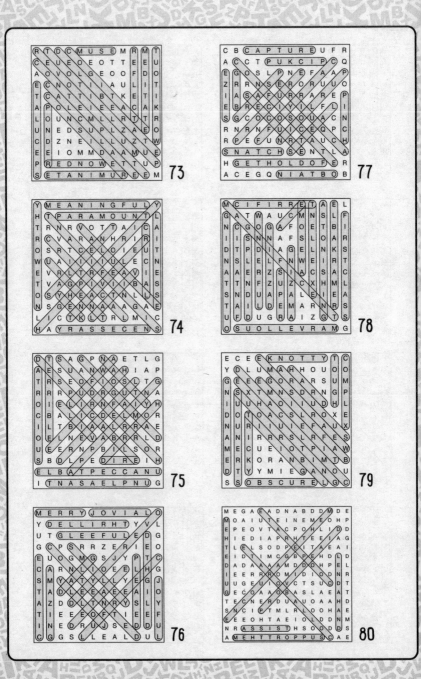

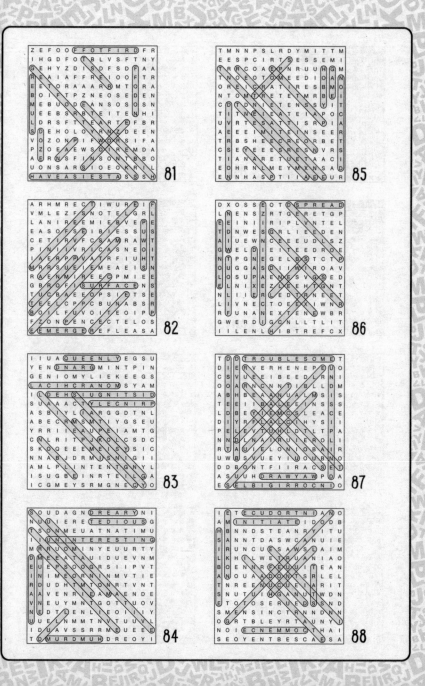

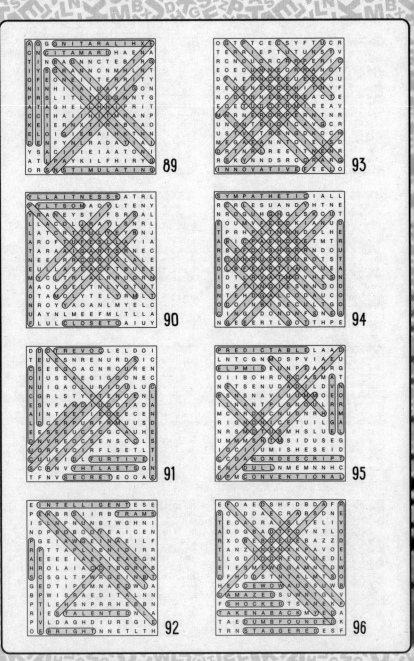

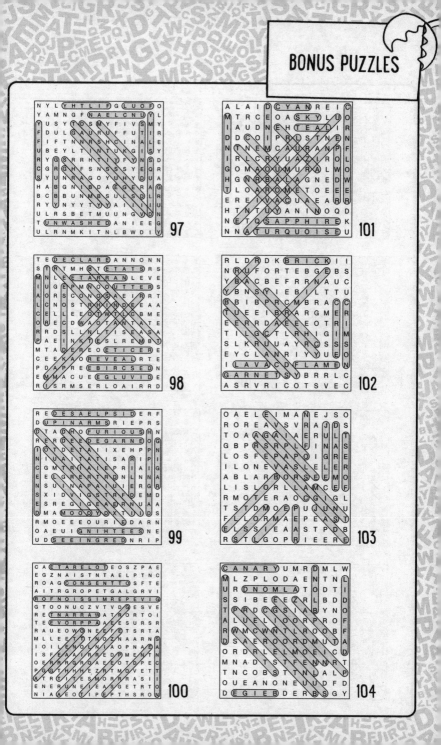

BONUS PUZZLES

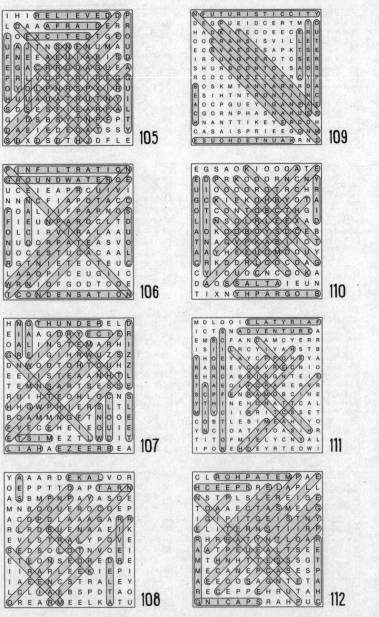

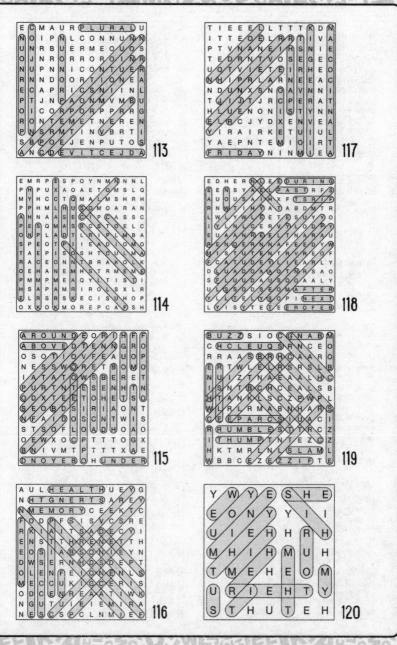

121

122

123

124

125

a) WEAR   e) PEAR
b) BEEN   f) FOUR
c) TAIL   g) MOUSSE
d) STATIONERY   h) THERE

126

a) BOARD   e) KNEAD
b) ATE   f) ADDITION
c) BAND   g) EWES
d) FLOUR   h) WRITE

127

a) MANE   e) SENT
b) TOAD   f) POUR
c) WON   g) CEILING
d) CHORD   h) I'LL

128

```
A U L K M X E M F F
A R R M T I E E H A
P M N E A P S I T Y
E B U E A R E S T H
H C R A E T E C E C
O E E E H F L N X D
L G T G A H F M T E
Y H U Y A K E E C T
T A F X C A F R C E
C T G A T F X G A T
```

a) AREN'T   e) MEAT
b) EXCEPT   f) BREAK
c) CAUGHT   g) HOLY
d) EFFECT   h) MISSED

129

```
J D L V Q S N U N Q
J S L W A B Z B D H
L W T I A D N W R C
L E H G O H E E F Z
W A E E Q D I W M U
E X E H T G F X O K
S Y Y R N H T G I M
P V T F C S E I F V
C T I A N V C R A F
G W X O K T X Q A W
```

a) MOWED   e) WHETHER
b) REIGN   f) REAL
c) HEEL   g) WAIT
d) SEW   h) BAWL

130

```
B A G G W G R E A T
H A S H O E I A D A
R E T D R G H I I E
H H W T P A E T H D
R D I S A B A A H A
A R T A A R V R G A
A C P O D A A A R E
C B H D A E E A I I
H W E A H I E A A N
O I R R T B I E O H
```

a) BEAR   e) OAR
b) PAST   f) HEAR
c) RODE   g) VAIN
d) WITCH   h) GREAT

131

```
Y S S A E D D S S L L A
L E U Y R A U R B E F N
R S L R M O M D I S F S
I D F D P N F E I R D S
I Y R F I R E L S S R E
Y N D E G F I P I O S R
D T T E I R F S O R L D
S R L E S S A I E R N D
R I S I R E E M C S S A
T S T A D E R D M U F R
R S S S L C S T E A L I
R B F R F E A T R L R T
```

a) LOSE   e) FEBRUARY
b) DESERT   f) GRAMMAR
c) ADDRESS   g) INTEREST
d) SURPRISE   h) DIFFICULT

132

```
D E D P O T A T O E S N
I E C E C L E L S I Y D
N M T A F C L F I R T N
T B S N S I N B A N A R
E A R E I N N S S L A R
L R F A P O S X I M E A
L R S S R E P O T R M T
I A T S C A S P C E I R
G S A E L T E T A R L N
E N C P C E P S N I L
T D N D E D D R L E A D
```

a) ARCTIC   e) DEFINITELY
b) POTATOES   f) DISAPPOINTED
c) NECESSARY   g) EMBARRASSED
d) INTELLIGENT   h) ALMOST

133

```
E F A T L L N R Y E N D
G R L C Q E Y I C L G A
R F E E H L I A G N H T
A N L R E I A L I D N F
T Q T L E R E N N E R A
E N L E F I T V R I F A
F U F D O H G E E R Y D
U N E U G H F N E E E N
L O E I R F D L R A R E
H U L F I I R U F L Q L
E G E D A U I H D L F A
N E T E Y A L A U Y E C
```

a) ACHIEVE   e) REALLY
b) FRIEND   f) GRATEFUL
c) QUEUE   g) LIGHTNING
d) DIFFERENT   h) CALENDAR

134

```
O M P L U O N
H O O T O A O
T P M E P A S
M U W N L W A
G N O A W O W
O U H O N A W
O M N S L S T
```

135

```
W E A A A W S
A S K A E L D
N E O S O E S
D A N R C P I
S I E I E A N
P C W M A W K
E E A A A S E
```

136

```
T R A P W I A
R A L E S F N
R R A I W R E
L K N O A S L
A G L C O E O
T B E H A L T
E F P F E C R
```

137

```
S G N I W M K
E O O L E N S
S R S L I S T
O A O T T O O
L N S H A W O
V I I W S O L
E E R H T O G
```

138

```
I R Y I O P S R P S
R O L F S E E F E I
E E T E T A I T R S
C Y A A C N O P M S
N P R T I M R L I E
I I I S E R E A S L
P O H R P I E Y S N
N E I R A R N E I I
D P L P P P S R N A
E P P E H P A S P
```

139

```
F R A G R E E E B E
G R H E G I E N I H
G R E E E R E O G T
E E E M F F U R R H
O F R G E T N D T G
F A T R S M G F N I
S S E I R O B O E N
F A D E E N R E F E
N E R O B T R A R D
A F F N S T F A F R
```

a) STRONG   e) OUTSIDE
b) FREE   f) SAFE
c) FAR   g) REMEMBER
d) NIGHT   h) AGREE

140

```
U U L B L N K D U K
V E F E A Y R I E N
N E S N V R A R E I
Y V W S W E D T U F
N A I I E I N Y N O
D R Y U B N T N O U
D B E N E L I R N N
Y I Y A I U U L R D
G A L U K O I I G N
E S G E E G A N N U
```

a) UGLINESS   e) DARK
b) BRAVE   f) DAWN
c) DIRTY   g) FOUND
d) EVEN   h) GUILTY

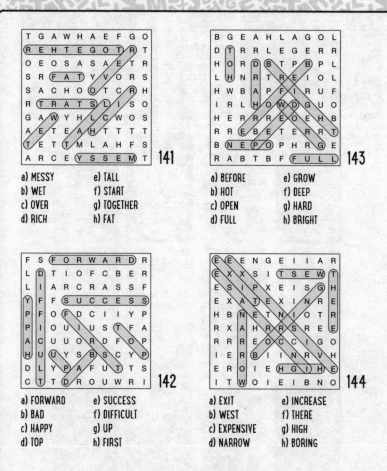

141

a) MESSY
b) WET
c) OVER
d) RICH
e) TALL
f) START
g) TOGETHER
h) FAT

143

a) BEFORE
b) HOT
c) OPEN
d) FULL
e) GROW
f) DEEP
g) HARD
h) BRIGHT

142

a) FORWARD
b) BAD
c) HAPPY
d) TOP
e) SUCCESS
f) DIFFICULT
g) UP
h) FIRST

144

a) EXIT
b) WEST
c) EXPENSIVE
d) NARROW
e) INCREASE
f) THERE
g) HIGH
h) BORING

Introducing the Wordsearch Master:
Gareth Moore. B.Sc (Hons) M.Phil Ph.D

Dr Gareth Moore is an Ace Puzzler, and author
of lots of puzzle and brain-training books.

He created an online brain-training site called BrainedUp.com,
and runs an online puzzle site called PuzzleMix.com. Gareth has
a Ph.D from the University of Cambridge, where he taught
machines to understand spoken English.

ALSO AVAILABLE:

ISBN 9781780558721

ISBN 9781780558738

ISBN 9781780557403

ISBN 9781780557106

ISBN 9781780556659

ISBN 9781780556642

ISBN 9781780556635

ISBN 9781780556628

ISBN 9781780556543

ISBN 9781780556192

ISBN 9781780556208

ISBN 9781780555935

ISBN 9781780555638

ISBN 9781780554730

ISBN 9781780555621

ISBN 9781780554723

ISBN 9781780555409

ISBN 9781780553146

ISBN 9781780553085

ISBN 9781780553078

ISBN 9781780552491